SALON PSYCHOLOGY

HOW TO SUCCEED WITH PEOPLE AND BE A POSITIVE PERSON

By **Dr. Lewis E. Losoncy**

Foreword by Arnold M. Miller, Founder, Matrix University

Matrix University Press, Solon, Ohio

© 1988 Matrix University Press

Library of Congress catalog card number: 87-63500
ISBN 0-9619951-0-6

Matrix University Press
30601 Carter Street
Solon, Ohio 44139

Printed in the United States of America

681006

THIS BOOK IS FONDLY DEDICATED...

TO YOU, THE SALON PROFESSIONAL, for all the times you have helped — from soothing the "first-haircut" fears to creating special styles for a golden anniversary. And for all those touching times in between. The world is finally opening its eyes to your contributions. YOUR DAY HAS COME.

TO YOU, THE MATRIX FIELD STAFF AND MATRIX DISTRIBUTOR FIELD STAFF, for caring so much about the stylists you serve. By encouraging them to attend Matrix University, you've helped them for a lifetime. Together, you've walked up the mountainside. Together, you've earned a fresher, richer perspective.

TO ALL OF YOU AT MATRIX ESSENTIALS, who touch the world by your daily contributions. You are the greatest group of people I have ever worked with. Like a seed in search of a place to grow, I would have been different without your find-a-way spirit.

TO YOU, ARNIE MILLER, whom history will record as the one voice who led the worldwide community of hairstylists forward into a new era. You ushered in the new day when you founded Matrix University, thus showing your fellow cosmetologists how much you believed in them. Because of your dreams, the dreams of an entire profession are now becoming reality.

I thank all of you for letting me, an outsider, in to sing my songs of psychology. It's been a perfect synergy of your world and mine.

FOREWORD

When I was twelve years old, I worked as a concession vender at the Cleveland Stadium. My view of the world was from the left-field bleachers, and I sometimes thought how lucky the other twelve-year-olds were who had a legitimate ticket and a seat.

I was there carrying Coke bottles up and down the concrete stairs. I knew then that I wanted to "find a way" so that I, too, could one day have a legitimate ticket and a seat.

I recall that experience now because it was my first introduction to motivation — motivation by a guy named Jack. To a twelve-year-old, Jack looked like a giant with burly arms. He scared the heck out of all the kids, including me. He would stand at the bottom of the left-field bleachers and deliver his pregame motivational message.

"You guys get out there and hustle. If you don't want to hustle, don't bother coming back to the next game. Get out and sell those Cokes while they're cold."

On cold days he would say, "They don't want cold hot chocolate — they want *hot* hot chocolate, so get out there and hustle and get that chocolate to them while it's still hot."

As I look back, I realize that Jack understood two things: (1) client satisfaction and (2) how to motivate venders.

I've been in the beauty industry for more than thirty years as a hairdresser, salon owner, and manufacturer. I am still working to give client satisfaction and still looking to motivate myself and others around me.

A few years ago I met Dr. Lewis Losoncy. I quickly learned that Dr. Lew understands our clients' needs and our professional needs better than anyone else in the world. He truly understands that a client comes to a salon to look better and feel better. I have believed this for years. Dr. Lew not only understands it but teaches us why.

Dr. Lew has combined the two fields of psychology and cosmetology into a new field called "Salon Psychology." He has helped thousands of professional cosmetologists understand their clients better. He has helped us take pride in what we do and have more confidence in ourselves. He has helped us grow both as professionals and as people.

This book is the first of its kind and will be the standard for future generations of professional cosmetologists. It is the basis of the Salon Psychology courses taught by Dr. Lew at Matrix University. He has already changed the destinies and determinations of thousands of stylists. He has taken the rudimentary, grass-roots motivation of a Jack at the Cleveland Stadium to a new level of understanding and professionalism for our industry.

As president and founder of Matrix Essentials, I want this book to help take the level of professional cosmetology to an even higher plateau. I want hairdressers to be recognized for the good that we do in helping hundreds of thousands of clients. I want us to better understand and rejoice in the clients we have touched and changed. It might seem that we alter only their appearance, but we truly alter the way they feel and the way other people feel about them. We give them confidence and therefore play an important part in their lives. We sometimes even alter their destinies.

I am proud to be a professional cosmetologist. My focus at Matrix is on you, the professional stylist, and the future of our industry. My focus is not only on developing quality products but on helping you become a sensitive, responsive professional who offers awareness, skills, and a touching hand to reveal your clients' inner and outer beauty.

My view of the world today is no longer just from the left-field bleachers. My view of the world is the result of many years spent behind the chair, touching and being touched by clients. So if I may offer one bit of encouragement, it is this — let's go up those stadium stairs together. The crowd is waiting. Let's hustle and offer clients the skills and sensitivity they are longing for. Let's find a way together. The rewards will far exceed the effort.

ARNOLD M. MILLER

Arnold M. Miller is a hairdresser, salon owner, platform artist, and educator. He is also president of Matrix Essentials, Inc., a manufacturer of exclusively professional hair-care products. Matrix University is his personal vision of a brighter future for professional cosmetologists worldwide.

PREFACE

CAN YOU REMEMBER *YOUR BEST MOMENT* AS A HAIRSTYLIST?
(If so take a few seconds to relive the experience.)

As you reflect on your best moment as a stylist or as a student in beauty school and its good feelings, ask yourself, "Were my good feelings about *hair,* or were my good feelings about my impact on another *person?*" Was another person involved in *YOUR BEST MOMENT?* I'll just bet that you would like to feel that way more often. *YOU CAN!*

Now allow your mind to reflect on a past moment in the salon that was the most stressful or frustrating moment, a moment when you wanted to give up, scream your heart out, or just cry for the rest of your life, alone! Relive it briefly.

Tough, wasn't it? I'll bet this negative emotional scene has something in common with the first one, the positive one. I'll bet this scene also had a *person* in it. Maybe this one didn't even involve *hair,* but I know it involved *PEOPLE.* Bet you'd like to avoid those frustrating days in the future. *YOU CAN!*

Isn't it interesting that your best and toughest moments in the salon were, and still are, moments with *PEOPLE?*

You are, or soon will be, a licensed cosmetologist who works on and with *PEOPLE.* Isn't it about time you were given *PEOPLE SKILLS* to complement your hair skills? . . . so that you can repeat good days and eliminate bad days.

In this book you will learn how to be successful with the most important part of your life and work — the *PEOPLE* part.

WHAT THIS BOOK CAN DO FOR YOU
Salon Psychology is divided into four parts.

Part I includes six interesting chapters to give you the skills and attitudes that will provide the winning edge with people in our High-Tech/High-Touch society of today and tomorrow. Rating scales from 1.0 to 5.0 are included in these chapters to measure and improve your levels in all of the six important categories. Exercises are also included to help you achieve excellence in each area. You will learn how to:

- Have the right things to say when people talk.

- Avoid being put into the position of trying to solve a client's problems.

- Help every one of your clients to seek out every salon benefit you have to offer.

- Give such good service to people that they will comment on how great you make them feel.

- Keep a positive attitude, every day, and be the salon stimulant.

- Immediately start a campaign to retain and expand your clientele.

You will never be the same, and people will be noticing the changes in you almost immediately!

Part II comprises stimulating ideas from people who are experts on why people act the way they do. You will learn how you can:

- Understand why sometimes people do things that don't consciously make sense.

- Draw powers from unconscious sources within you to create new strengths for the day.

- Deal with a disruptive child or a nagging client by understanding what they are really saying.

- Understand how changing a hairstyle creates anxiety for some clients and how to help them overcome their doubts.

- Design a High-Touch salon environment that sends out winning vibes to your clients.

- Unfailingly cope with stresses and pressures that before would have dragged you down.

Part II will give you an excellent personality theory background to prepare you for Part III, the practical part of dealing with people.

Part III discusses five different types of people who come into the salon and shows how, by using the theory from Part II, you can succeed with all types of people. You will learn how to:

- Deal with the client who tries to "put you down."

- Bring out the shy client who doesn't give any clues as to how she wants her hair cut.

- Be effective with a loud person who is constantly seeking your attention.

This practical part of the book will make your life with others easier and more fulfilling. You will be much better equipped to cope with the people part of your work after reading these chapters.

Part IV is an uplifting gift of encouragement and motivation — all for you. You will learn how to:

- Develop ways to keep yourself continuously motivated.

- Become a *FIND-A-WAY* to your ultimate dreams *PERSON*.

You will learn these and many other skills and attitudes that will lead to more Ultimate Moments in your professional and personal life.

Lewis E. Losoncy, Ph.D.

CONTENTS

INTRODUCTION
A Choice Time for Salon Professionals

The times "they are a-changing." A changing world is dramatically reshaping businesses and especially the way professionals — doctors, dentists, and cosmetologists — are approaching people. The time of the indifferent treatment of a client is giving way to the concept of the "new, encouraging professional."

In today's demanding and changing world, the cosmetology profession is hungry for new knowledge, new skills in dealing with people, coworkers, and even self. Standing on the welcome mat of the twenty-first century, we find that client sensitivity is as important as chemical science. Indeed, in a previous work, *The Motivating Leader,* I called this "The Age of Encouragement." It is a time when successful professionals will have people skills, a people-oriented attitude, and service sensitivity to individuals. The echoes of this changing society have never been heard so clearly by those in the service professions as they are today.

John Naisbitt's bestseller, *Megatrends,* shows very convincingly that people today are more aware of their options to choose among professionals and are more assertive than ever in using those options. While the 1950s family would rarely leave either their family doctor or barber, the family of the twenty-first century flocks to the most sensitive doctor or stylist with the best skills. We are truly living in what Naisbitt calls the "Era of High Tech/High Touch."

In their book, *Service America,* Karl Albrecht and Ron Zemke call our time "The Age of Service" and tell us that good human-relations service provides the competitive edge . . . and will be even more important in the future.

THE COSMETOLOGY PROFESSION IS CHANGING BY DEVELOPING PEOPLE SKILLS

This newly aware and assertive consumer arrived without knocking, and many professions did not know how to make their guest welcome. Cosmetologists can be proud that it was their profession that responded first to the new consumer by providing a relevant education for its professionals. Our new form of education is sensitive to the importance of the High-Touch component of "High Tech/High Touch." *PEOPLE KNOWLEDGE, PEOPLE SKILLS!*

The new form of education is called *Salon Psychology: a study of how the fields of psychology and human relations can be applied to achieving success with the "people" part of the salon.*

Salon Psychology is designed to fulfill the total needs of the cosmetologist. In a sense this book could be called a motivation book, and no doubt anyone who works his or her way between its covers will feel a continuous surge of pride. But it is even more. The wisdom living in these pages is in the form of skills that are long lasting and steeped in the behavioral sciences, the sciences of people.

At its deepest level, isn't the hairstyling profession as much related to people as it is to hair? Are not hairstyles based upon the lifestyles of people? More stylists leave salons — and their profession — for people reasons than for hair reasons, and more clients pick their stylists for people reasons (attitude, communication) than for hair reasons. As a psychologist who has studied the hairstyling profession for more than a dozen years, I realized how important the "people part" of the salon was. And yet most stylists had received no formal training in dealing with clients, coworkers, or even the stresses that they themselves experienced daily. I had a rare opportunity to observe from an outsider's perspective the importance of the cosmetology profession on our society. I have written this book to provide not only the necessary people skills stylists need to actualize their potential but to communicate my respect, love, and enthusiasm for the cosmetology profession.

This book lays the foundation for the new direction of the salon profession. The study of Salon Psychology was initiated by Arnold Miller, president of Matrix Essentials, a hairstylist himself, who wanted all cosmetologists in the world to have the education they need to be as successful as their dreams will allow. Without his determination and vision, this book would not have become a reality.

Indeed the times "they are a-changing," and the changes are positive ones of tremendous and unprecedented opportunity for anyone who chooses to be part of the new wave. That is why *Salon Psychology* sees today and tomorrow as a *Choice Time* for the cosmetology profession.

CHOOSE to be part of the new momentum!

You can start by developing the six most important skills and attitudes to give you the cutting edge.

L.E.L.

PART I

SKILLS AND ATTITUDES TO GIVE YOU THE CUTTING EDGE

The six chapters in Part I give you the six master keys to open doors for success with people in the salon.

CHAPTER 1

TURNING PEOPLE ON WITH HIGH-TOUCH EMPATHY

Real contact with another person is perhaps the most exciting thing we experience in life. That contact is called communication. Communication is the most vital component of the stylist-client relationship. A stylist cannot "not communicate" with her client. Silence communicates as strongly as continuous talk. The way the stylist touches, moves, and responds communicates a message. Clients choose their stylist based upon his or her communication skills. This chapter is designed to help you communicate more empathically to turn your clients on to themselves and to your work.

Soon You Will Be Able To:

- Be the kind of person whom clients want to select all the time.

- Feel comfortable with almost any person, any time.

- Know how to really listen to other people and understand them.

- Avoid the trap of feeling you have to solve peoples' personal problems.

HIGH-TOUCH EMPATHY

Compare these different stylists' responses to a client's statement.

Client: Guess what, I became a grandmother last week!

First Stylist: Oh, that's nothing — I have been a grandmother ten times already. Let me tell you about my grandchildren.

Second Stylist: A grandmother for the first time! How exciting that must be for you. Can you bring me a picture of your grandchild next time?

Which stylist has better human-relations skills? If both of these stylists have equal cutting abilities, which one do you think will have a bigger following? The answer, obviously, is the second stylist. The second stylist has High-Touch Empathy, the single most important people skill for success.

In this chapter you are going to learn all about empathy, and you will develop your skill in listening and responding.

With empathy, you will not only be more effective and popular with clients, but also with coworkers, family, and friends.

WHAT IS HIGH-TOUCH EMPATHY?

Empathy is the willingness and ability to see the world through the eyes of another, to hear the world through the ears of another, and to feel the world with the heart of another. Empathy is like walking a mile in another person's shoes. Empathy is the skill of really listening to understand. Empathic communication is the skill of responding in a way that communicates that understanding.

Another way to perceive this important skill of empathy is to contrast what empathy is with what empathy isn't.

What empathy is not

1. Empathy is not trying to outdo someone by playing "Can you top this?" with her.

2. Empathy is not trying to judge people.

What empathy is

1. Empathy is trying to understand someone's feelings.

2. Empathy is trying to see the person's world from her perspective.

For example:

> **Client:** My husband is a Republican and I am a Democrat.
>
> **Stylist:** I agree with your husband.

> **Client:** My husband is a Republican and I am a Democrat.
>
> **Stylist:** Sounds as if there must be some interesting discussions at your house.

3. Empathy is not trying to solve people's problems.

3. Empathy is communicating back to clients their feelings.

Add some of your own ideas as to what empathy is not and what empathy is. Consider things like how you can tell when people are in tune with you and how you can tell when they aren't. Include factors like the way they look, their body language, mannerisms, and what they say.

What empathy is not

_____

_____

_____

_____

_____

What empathy is

_____

_____

_____

_____

_____

MEASURING A STYLIST'S LEVELS OF HIGH-TOUCH EMPATHY

There are good cuts and bad cuts. There are good ways to communicate and bad ways. The great news is that we are able to measure good communication skills.

To measure your levels of empathy, take a look at the Stylist Empathy Rating Scale; then evaluate the responses that follow from a low-level response at 1.0 (poor communication) to an ultimate high level of empathic communication at 5.0 on the scale. The average is 3.0.

In the next few minutes, you will understand exactly what it is that effective communicators know and do.

STYLIST EMPATHY RATING SCALE

1.0 No stylist-client interaction except "How do you want your hair cut?" (No touch)

2.0 Stylist-client talk is on externals: soaps, weather, etc. (Fringe-contact with client)

3.0 Stylist talks about self: 1) "What you said reminds me of . . ." 2) Stylist talks more than 80% of the time, or 3) Stylist judges — "You're right" or "You're wrong."

4.0 Client talks; stylist listens, stays on the topic, but ignores feelings of client. Better than 3.0 because client is talking, but relationship isn't maximized because client's feelings are ignored.

5.0 Stylist listens for the client's feelings and shares them. By being understood *AT A FEELING LEVEL, CLIENT FEELS COMFORTABLE, SAFE, AND TRUSTED.* The stylist now learns more about the client's lifestyle and can make better recommendations. Stylist earns the right to be a consultant to the client's cosmetology needs.

Study the scale until you feel you are ready to rate some typical stylist responses to client statements. Notice that 5.0 responses — the best — include identifying the feelings behind the client's words and sharing them.

Imagine a person's saying the same thing to three different stylists and receiving three different answers. Go back to your rating scale and give each stylist response an empathic communications rating.

Client: I'm afraid of coloring my hair. I don't know how my husband will take to it.

First Stylist: Oh, that reminds me of the time that my husband told me what to do and I told him where to go.

Your rating _____

Second Stylist: How does your husband like your hair?

Your rating _____

Third Stylist: Like all good, new experiences, the first time somebody gets color, it's a bit scary. You're feeling a little uncertain about how your husband will respond. But underneath, you sound as if you could get excited about a new look. Perhaps your husband will sense your excitement.

Your rating _____

Just as you once learned to master perming or coloring, you can master High-Touch Empathy. It may be a little difficult at first, but soon these skills will be an important part of your life. Let's look at your ratings. The first stylist turned her client off by ignoring her world and immediately talking about self. That is a 3.0 rating. Check the Rating Scale again to see why this response is at a 3.0 level.

The second stylist stayed on the topic of the husband, which was great — but unfortunately she ignored the feelings of the client. That's a 4.0 rating. Can you see why?

The quality of the third stylist's response was rich. Notice the feeling words: scary, uncertain, get excited. That is clearly a 5.0 High-Touch Empathic response. Study these examples until you feel comfortable with the rating scale.

LISTENING FOR FEELINGS TO TURN PEOPLE ON!

Obviously, by looking at the scale we can see how important it is to relate to people — not by judging, dominating, ignoring, or taking responsibility for the client's personal problems, but by tuning in to people's feelings. Most of the world does not do this, and that is why, when someone does, people really respond. To help you tune in to feelings, here is a list of feelings that you can use for starters.

Negative Feelings

Worried, angry, fed up, irritated, bored, confused, let down, worthless, disgusted, uncertain, unsure, embarrassed, humiliated, frustrated, guilty, rotten, hurt, picked on, not sure of yourself, grumpy, jealous, put down, left out, sad, unhappy, down, shocked.

Positive Feelings

Respected, valued, important, appreciated, brave, confident, sure of yourself, comfortable, secure, caring, determined, encouraged, thrilled, glad, great, terrific, grateful, inspired, loved, proud, relieved, surprised, trusted.

HOW TO LISTEN AND RESPOND EMPATHICALLY

An effective way to learn to respond empathically is to start a response off with:

You feel (apply a feeling word) because (give the reason).

Now it's your turn to develop your skill of High-Touch Empathy. You have studied the rating scale and have looked over a list of feeling words. Here is your opportunity to put to use the most important people skill of them all — empathic listening and responding.

In each of the following three situations, someone says something to you. In the first case it's a client; in the second instance it is another stylist; and in the third example it is a manager.

Write what you would say back to them. Remember:

1. Look at the High-Touch Empathy Scale.

2. Find a feeling word from the negative or positive feelings list and select a feeling you believe the person is experiencing.

3. Keep yourself out of it. No judging.

4. Do not take responsibility to give an answer or solve someone's problem. Simply share a feeling that you think she may be experiencing.

>**Client says to you:** It was our fifth wedding anniversary yesterday and my husband didn't even remember.

>**Respond:** (Check rating scale; find a feeling from the negative or positive list of feelings.)

>You feel _____

>because _____

>**Another stylist says to you:** I used to feel important around here until this new stylist came. Now the manager spends so much time with her.

>**Respond:**

>You feel _____

>because _____

>**Manager says to you:** I'm really in the middle. The owner puts pressure on me, and you guys seem to be ganging up on me. I don't know what to do — it's not like before when I was styling. Since I got the promotion, I've lost all my friends.

>**Respond:**

>You feel _____

>because _____

Do all of your answers include feeling words? Did you stay on the topic? Did you keep yourself out? Did you avoid giving advice or judging? If so, congratulations. If not, take a few seconds and write a different response. You can do it! You have just learned the most important skill that people who work with people need — High-Touch Empathy.

HIGH-TOUCH EMPATHY VS. APATHY OR SYMPATHY

Don't make your livelihood more demanding than it is. Avoid burnout by communicating with High-Touch Empathy, and avoid the apathy and sympathy traps.

Clients, like stylists, have families, friends, joys, and problems. In a world that frequently doesn't seem to care, anyone who finds even a slightly open door to bring his or her problems through will do so.

Sometimes without even knowing it, people burden others. This is especially true of some salon clients who feel close to their stylists in that touching relationship. The close contact between stylist and client involves human touch and even "washing the mask away." The salon provides an atmosphere that sends out a natural invitation for a person to unload. Not only can she get her hair done by a caring individual, but she finds someone who will listen.

In this chapter on listening and responding, it becomes vital to understand what effective, empathic listening is, as well as what it is not. The right kind of listening — empathic listening — builds a relationship between client and stylist and is a very important human-relations skill. But the wrong kind of listening — apathetic or sympathetic — either destroys relationships or puts the stylist in a role he or she isn't prepared for. Before we discuss effective listening, let's examine the two ineffective listening and responding styles.

APATHETIC-RESPONDING STYLIST

Client: I know I don't have an appointment and you're booked solid, but I'd like to have a perm because I'm going to see my son tomorrow. He's coming home from the service, and I haven't seen him for almost two years.

Stylist: (Apathetic response) I don't have any time.

The stylist totally ignores the client's personal concerns. There are obviously some real feelings that this woman is experiencing, and the stylist sweeps them under the rug. It certainly wouldn't be hard for an empathic stylist to win this client over, would it?

Sympathetic over-involvement, the next type of response, is the opposite of apathetic non-caring.

SYMPATHETIC-RESPONDING STYLIST

Client: I know I don't have an appointment and you are booked solid, but I'd like to have a perm because I'm going to see my son tomorrow. He's coming home from the service, and I haven't seen him for almost two years.

Stylist: (Sympathetic response) I had a class I was going to tonight, but I'll cancel out and do your hair. I'll even bake you a cake for tomorrow. The perm is on me.

The main reason stylists burn out on the job, go home, take the telephone off the hook, and close themselves from the outside world is that they overinvest themselves with *SYMPATHETIC LISTENING* and *RESPONDING*.

The cosmetologist is not responsible for solving people's problems. The stylist is not a psychiatrist, psychologist, or social worker. The cosmetologist is an expert on hair, skin, and nails. Just as a psychiatrist with shears and comb would be inappropriate, a stylist's positon becomes inappropriate the moment she allows a client to put her in a "solve my problem" situation.

A cosmetologist takes a huge burden off her own shoulders the minute she clearly faces this fact: I do not have to solve my client's problem; it is not my responsibility. But then what do you do when people bring their problems to you?

EMPATHIC-RESPONDING STYLIST

Client: I know I don't have an appointment and you are booked solid, but I'd like to have a perm because I am going to see my son tomorrow. He's coming home from the service, and I haven't seen him for almost two years.

Stylist: (Empathic response) You must feel really excited about seeing your son after almost two years. I'll bet you can't wait. Let me check my book to see if there is any possible way I can give you a perm. . . . I'm sorry, Mrs. Smith, I can't. I know that must be really disappointing to you. Maybe one of our other stylists can help.

Empathic responding involves tuning in to a person's feelings. The reasons a stylist uses empathic responding are that (1) it builds rapport; (2) 68 percent of clients say they choose stylists for human, not technical, skills; (3) when a client feels a good, safe relationship, she shares more about herself, which aids in understanding her lifestyle, thus enabling the stylist to better understand the client's needs.

TWO STYLIST-CLIENT DIALOGUES COMPARING SYMPATHETIC VS. EMPATHIC LISTENING AND RESPONDING

Sympathetic-Responding Stylist

Client: My husband is in danger of losing his job.

Sympathetic stylist: Well, let me see if I know anyone who is hiring.

Client: And my teenager is having a problem at school.

Sympathetic stylist: Did you talk to the principal?

Client: No.

Sympathetic stylist: What about his teacher?

Client: No.

Sympathetic stylist: Well, I know the school counselor. Let me talk to her.

Client: My in-laws are coming for dinner Sunday, and I just feel so inferior about my cooking.

Sympathetic stylist: I'm baking lasagna Saturday. Let me bring you some.

Empathic-Responding Stylist

A person with a 5.0 level on the High-Touch Scale understands and shares back the feelings of another person — but stops there.

Observe how an empathic stylist would listen to the same client.

Client: My husband is in danger of losing his job.

Empathic stylist: You feel a little up in the air now, I guess, because of your husband's uncertain future at work.

Client: And my teenager is having a problem at school.

Empathic stylist: You're worried about Jimmy.

Client: I've been so depressed lately.

Empathic stylist: Things are really difficult now. I'll bet you're waiting for things to turn around.

Client: Yeah.

Empathic stylist: Maybe we can start here, with a new style. That always gives a person a lift!

Notice that the stylist did not get caught in the "solve my problem" trap but just listened for feelings — even more effective and without the emotional drain.

The three listening styles are contrasted below:

Apathetic Listening: Communicating that I am not interested in your feelings or your life. I'm just here to cut your hair.

Empathic Listening: Communicating that I am interested in understanding your feelings and sharing them with you. Yet I am fully aware that they are not my feelings and your world is not my world. We are two different people, and I can't possibly solve ten people's problems each day.

Sympathetic Listening: Communicating that not only am I interested in understanding your feelings and your world, but I'm going to move into your world and forget about my own. I'll find a way to solve your problems, and if I don't, I'll feel guilty.

TURN PEOPLE ON WITH
5.0 HIGH-TOUCH EMPATHY

1. The next time you are in a situation where you feel insecure about not having an answer to someone's problem, feel secure that you don't have to. Simply share back to them the feelings behind their words. Feel good!

2. The next time you are in a situation with a client where you feel apathetic, listen for feelings and share them back. You'll see how simple it is. Feel good!

3. Since clients choose their stylists based upon High Touch as well as High Tech, this skill of empathic response to feelings is the key to turning people on. Feel good!

Now, let's see how you can take your turned-on clients to new levels with High-Tech Designing.

CHAPTER 2

TAKING YOUR CLIENTS TO NEW LEVELS WITH HIGH-TECH BENEFITS

As a stylist with 5.0 High-Touch Empathy, you turn clients on. By helping these turned-on clients receive every benefit you offer, you will keep them. You have so many gifts to give. In this chapter we will talk about how to maximize your clients' appearance by offering them the 5 C's — cut, color, curl, condition, and continuation of service. You will also learn how to offer your best technical benefits to every client. In the era of High Tech/High Touch, you can become the ultimate 5.0 High-Tech/5.0 High-Touch stylist.

Soon You Will Be Able To:

- Help every client realize all of the benefits you can give.

- Be seen as the cosmetic expert in your clients' eyes.

- Measure your level of High-Tech benefits and improve on them immediately.

HIGH-TECH BENEFITS FOR CLIENTS

We have just talked about the vital skill of *EMPATHY,* your *KEY* to *TURNING PEOPLE ON. HIGH-TOUCH EMPATHY* links you with people in a bond that exists as long as your High-Touch Empathy exists. High-Touch Empathy builds trust, good communication, and mutual understanding. That's what you want from your doctor, dentist, and lawyer. And that's what people want from you. They will make you successful if you satisfy their need to feel important and understood.

Once the High-Touch relationship is created with your client, she feels a bond of trust and respect for you. She looks to you as an expert. She has, in most instances, chosen you out of many stylists. Your client looks to you, as an expert, to assist her in looking her very best through your technical skills, advice, and recommendations.

We encourage you to think about each of your clients, one by one, and ask yourself if you are helping each one to receive all the benefits from the salon that he or she could.

I know that when my patients came to me as their psychologist, they sought therapy in the hope of developing their inner image to its fullest potential. Some had no idea where to start; others had thought about ways to improve themselves a bit, while others had read self-help books and were already knowledgeable about how to bring out their best. But these three types, at three different levels of awareness, had one thing in common: They all looked to their psychologist as the expert, the one with the specialized education, the one who could give additional knowledge, skills, and recommendations in addition to what they already knew.

If a client comes to a psychologist and the psychologist adds nothing — no new recommendations, suggestions, or ideas — in a short period of time the client will find another who provides *additional recommendations and benefits.*

Some stylists ask the client how she wants her hair cut and, without any additional professional recommendations, simply cut her hair that way. Such stylists, well-intentioned though they may be, aren't adding to the client's knowledge and appearance. Unfortunately, they assume that the client understands all of the available technical services, skills, and products as well as the many different styles she can wear. Consequently, the client loses out because the stylist was not an additional source of consultation and recommendation. The client leaves with the same amount of knowledge she had when she came to the salon!

YOU ARE THE EXPERT

Keep in mind that no matter how much a client knows about hair, it is unlikely that he or she knows more than the stylist — a licensed professional who has studied the subject of hair care for hundreds of hours, who has attended education programs, and who stands behind the chair working with scores of people each week.

Just let your mind flow freely and think about all of the potential *HIGH-TECH GIFTS* you have to give to each of your clients! It's called the *ADDITIONAL POWER OF HIGH-TECH DESIGNING.* That means adding to your client's knowledge of hair, adding to your client's feelings of excitement about who she can be, and, mainly, adding to your client's appearance.

HOW TO BE A 5.0 HIGH-TECH DESIGNER AND GIVE ADDITIONAL POWER TO EACH AND EVERY CLIENT

You have developed the skill of 5.0 High-Touch Empathy by listening to the feelings behind your client's words. You understood her, made her feel comfortable and safe, and shared things about her lifestyle — all through *5.0 HIGH-TOUCH EMPATHY!*

Great news! It is also possible to become a *5.0 HIGH-TECH DESIGNER* by taking just a few minutes each day to think about the people you service. Giving additional power to each client every day builds you into a sought-after, successful stylist who, with the combination of High-Touch Empathy and High-Tech Designing, will rarely lose a client. Here is how to become a 5.0 High-Tech Designer:

STEP ONE:

Memorize these five services that will maximize the benefits your clients can receive from the salon.

CUT
COLOR
CURL
CONDITION
CONTINUATION OF SERVICE

STEP TWO:

List the names of the people you will be servicing today or on your next day in the salon. For example:

9:00	Mrs. Clark
9:30	Mr. Taylor
10:00	Mrs. Williamson
11:00	Ms. Monroe

STEP THREE:

Rate the *HIGH-TECH BENEFITS* you have given each person on your list during the last six months. You can determine the *HIGH-TECH DESIGNING ADDITIONAL BENEFITS* by looking again at Step One, the *Five C's of High-Tech Designing*. For example, your 9:00, Mrs. Clark. How many of those possible five C's have you suggested to her in the past five months? If you recommended a *cut*, a *curl*, a *condition*, and a *continuation of service* (which means products to help her maintain and enhance her hair at home), you score 4.0 in

High-Tech Designer Service. Great! Jot in your rating score beside Mrs. Clark's name. Then add the others by the same process.

9:00	Mrs. Clark	4.0 HIGH-TECH DESIGN
9:30	Mr. Taylor	1.0 HIGH-TECH DESIGN
10:00	Mrs. Williamson	2.0 HIGH-TECH DESIGN
11:00	Ms. Monroe	2.0 HIGH-TECH DESIGN

STEP FOUR:

Increase your additional power of benefits to your clients and your *HIGH-TECH DESIGN RATING* by looking over your list and asking yourself if you could raise the score for each person *ONE POINT* by recommending an additional benefit. For example, Mr. Taylor has received only one salon benefit, a cut. Perhaps you could recommend to Mr. Taylor a continuation of service, such as a professional shampoo and conditioner for use at home. Thus you help him receive an additional benefit from the salon, and it comes from you, his expert in hair.

STEP FIVE:

Set yourself a goal for today (or your next day in the salon). Measure your *HIGH-TECH DESIGN RATING* now compared to your rating before using the rating scale. If a client decides not to use a service you recommend, you *STILL SCORE* that rating point because you offered the additional benefit. (In those instances where a service is not relevant — for example, if you feel color is not appropriate for a certain client — certainly don't recommend it. And you automatically score the point because the recommendation wasn't appropriate.)

FEEL FREE TO USE THIS SHEET AND TO MAKE COPIES OF THIS HIGH-TECH DESIGN RATING SCALE

Stylist _____

Date _____

Client's Name	Previous High-Tech Rating	New Goal	Final Rating
1._____	_____	_____	_____
2._____	_____	_____	_____
3._____	_____	_____	_____
4._____	_____	_____	_____
5._____	_____	_____	_____
6._____	_____	_____	_____
7._____	_____	_____	_____
8._____	_____	_____	_____
9._____	_____	_____	_____
10._____	_____	_____	_____
11._____	_____	_____	_____
12._____	_____	_____	_____
13._____	_____	_____	_____
14._____	_____	_____	_____
15._____	_____	_____	_____
16._____	_____	_____	_____
17._____	_____	_____	_____
18._____	_____	_____	_____

Don't forget to reward yourself for higher-level achievement of High-Tech Designing. Feel a surge of professional pride, too. But your real satisfaction and fulfillment come from helping someone look and feel better by getting all of the salon benefits that you have to offer! *5.0 HIGH TECH/5.0 HIGH TOUCH NEVER LOSES A CLIENT!*

CHAPTER 3

AMAZING PEOPLE WITH YOUR SENSITIVITY TO SERVICE

A 5.0 High-Touch Empathy builds the relationship between you and the client; 5.0 High-Tech Designing builds you as the expert who can fill your client's cosmetic needs. A 5.0 service system in your salon rounds out a perfect experience for your clients. This chapter shows how to offer the ultimate salon service.

Soon You Will Be Able To:

- Project the ultimate service attitude to live by in order to assure yourself professional fulfillment and prosperity.

- Identify key service points in the total salon experience.

- Give service to people that will establish a loyalty to you as long as you give that service.

- Remove every single point of "potential hassle" for the client in his or her salon experience.

- Turn a dissatisfied, complaining customer into a cheerleader for your salon.

SERVICE:
THE OTHER SIDE OF THE CUTTING EDGE

Albert Schweitzer asserted that "there is no higher religion than human service." Albert Einstein stated that "the only reason we are here on earth is to be of service to one another." Alfred Adler, the noted psychiatrist of common sense, showed how serving others, or what he called "social interest," not only fulfills our need to contribute but lies at the very base of good mental health. Webster equates service with "usefulness," "benefits given to one another," or "a profession of respect communicated to another, like my service to you."

In his book, *Earl Nightingale's Greatest Discovery*, Nightingale argues convincingly that our life, our income, and our respect are directly related to how well we serve other people's needs and wants. In their bestseller, A *Passion for Excellence*, Tom Peters and Nancy Austin devote five full chapters to the importance of service to customers, clients, or patients. And in their perceptive book, *Service America*, Karl Albrecht and Ron Zemke have more than two hundred pages of material to prove that the differential competitive edge for any business today is service . . . and it will be even more important tomorrow! Serve people's wants and needs well, and they will return. It's that simple! In fact, *Roget's Thesaurus* associates the word "service" with the word "value." I show how much I value you by how well I serve you. If I value you and serve you better than anyone else, you will become my client and stay my client . . . until the moment someone else starts to value you more by providing better service than I do.

In his classic book, *The Magic of Thinking Big*, David Schwartz concludes on the topic of service, "The seed of money is service. Put service first and money takes care of itself. Always give people more than they expect to get. Each little extra thing you do for others is a money seed."

Jan Carlzon, president of Scandinavian Air Services (SAS) and author of *Moments of Truth*, states bluntly the importance of service: "Whenever an employee confronts the public, he creates a memorable impression that can determine whether the customer continues to do business with him or walks out the door. Last year each of our ten million passengers came in contact with five SAS employees, and this contact lasted an average of fifteen seconds. Thus SAS is created in the minds of our customers fifty million times a year, fifteen seconds at a time. These fifty million moments of truth determine the success or failure of our company."

At this moment you are making a commitment either to mediocrity or to excellence in service. On your decision, your future as a salon professional rests. You can do it!

This chapter on service may very well be the most important chapter in this book. Here we will look at how people sense a business' service attitude, how salon service can be measured, evaluated, and improved, and — most important — what you can do specifically at every service point in your salon to provide a positive, enriching, and memorable experience for your clients! Service is the other side of the cutting edge.

POSITIVE SERVICE ATTITUDE: SENSING THE SERVICE ATTITUDES OF A BUSINESS

In one restaurant, the service attitude of the business is reflected by a waitress who gets snappy at a customer because he requests a special order. In another restaurant only a few doors away, the menu and the waitress invite customers not to limit themselves to the menu but to think about what they are in the mood to eat. This restaurant, its employees, and its chef take enthusiastic pride in customer satisfaction. *Good service starts with customer needs and wants, not restaurant workers' or chefs' egos.* (Remember Rule #1 — The Customer Is Always Right.) This restaurant is service sensitive, and its people realize that while in most of their lives they are "receivers" of services and can demand, in this instance they are the "givers" of a service and now have to demand the best in themselves. You as a customer can sense the difference in service attitude very clearly, and in the future you will vote by selecting the restaurant that *acted with a positive service attitude that respected customers.*

CONTRASTING TWO SALONS' SERVICE ATTITUDES

Salon A. Clients enter with no one to greet them, are unsure where to put their coats, and sit in a dirty reception area, bored, waiting for service. The stylist takes personal phone calls on their time, talks about other clients, and offers them no new ideas on hairstyles or home care.

Salon B. Clients walk into a bright, cheerful environment where they get a friendly "Hello" from the receptionist that suggests "I'm glad to see you." That special person, the client, waits in a clean reception area with books and magazines depicting many different styles she could wear. She is reassured by a staff member that her wait will be brief and is even offered a cup of coffee or tea. Her stylist soon arrives, accompanies her to the first service, consults with her, and stays with her, sharing new styles, perms, colors, and a program of caring for her hair at home.

Over a period of time, which salon will be booming with clients? Again the answer is obvious — the salon with the Positive Service Attitude!

It is possible to observe, measure, and improve a salon's service attitude. Consider this Service-Attitude Rating Scale:

1.0 Service Attitude: Client viewed as an annoyance, made to apologize for any need or want she has, e.g., wants to talk about perms but the stylist rushes through the service, or needs to go to the bathroom but feels too intimidated to say so. No staff member smiles and client is ignored by stylists joking with each other.

2.0 Service Attitude: Client viewed with tolerance, a necessary evil. Staff sees her as a number, another head. She probably will not ask for additional services but if she does, will apologize.

3.0 Service Attitude: Treatment of client neither significantly positive or negative. Salon gives client what she says she wants, no more, no less. If client asks for additional services, the salon will comply.

4.0 Service Attitude: Salon team talks about the importance of servicing client's needs. All staff is sensitive, but salon has no established plan for all of the sensitive service points in the client's salon experience.

5.0 Service Superiority: Salon team has a formal plan to insure client comfort and convenience at every service point. Pride of service is felt by the total team.

We have discussed the importance of good service and establishing a Positive Service Attitude. We then listed a system to evaluate a salon's service attitude from a 1.0 to a 5.0 level. The biggest difference involved *HAVING A FORMAL PLAN* at every sensitive service point in the client's total salon experience. What are the nine key service points?

1) Salon Contact

2) Salon Entry

3) Reception Area and Pre-Service

4) Consultation

5) Shampooing

6) Technical Services and Recommendation

7) Client Reaction and Feedback from Services

8) Remuneration for Services

9) Staff-Supported Client Debut

Considering each of these service points, how can a salon create an atmosphere that guarantees a positive experience for every client, thus assuring success?

Let's study each service point separately and offer some suggestions to streamline salon service. You will then be encouraged to add any of your own service-sensitive ideas at each key point. We will study each service point by contrasting a 1.0 Service Attitude with a 5.0 Service Attitude.

SERVICE POINT 1: SALON CONTACT

The client's direct contact with the salon is either salon or client initiated. Many progressive salons are not waiting passively for people to seek out their services but *HAVE AN ACTIVE PLAN* to initiate contact with clients.

However, most salons place the responsibility for salon contact on the client. A person's direct contact with the salon occurs in two ways: either by walking in or by telephoning the salon for an appointment. Let's consider service to the client who contacts the salon by phone.

We'll contrast the 1.0 salon with the 5.0 salon and see how they treat the client on the telephone:

1.0 Salon Service	5.0 Salon Service
Long wait for phone to be answered; harsh, discourteous response.	Prompt response; pleasantly answered, enthusiastic tone.
Dull voice giving client vibes that salon couldn't care less.	Receptionist's voice gives feeling, "Glad you called, excited to hear from you."
Ignores name of client; doesn't introduce self.	Uses client's name frequently; makes sure client knows stylist by name.

| Cold, just-the-facts kind of treatment. | Builds anticipation about the salon, the staff, and the benefits; gets client excited about visit; says something special about stylist serving client. |
| Poor English or curt manner, e.g., "What do you want?" | Clearly articulated communications, e.g., "How may we be of service to you?" |

Salon contact, as you can see, is a vital service point because it sets the stage in the client's mind about the attitude of the salon. Many salons report first-time clients who call in to make an appointment do not show. In 90 percent of these cases, the reason is that the salon failed at this first service point.

Psychologically, people conclude that the attitudes and vibes they perceive in the person they speak to initially represent those of the total salon. Feel free to add any additional suggestions that a salon could use to improve its service at Service Point 1, salon contact:

_____

_____

_____

_____

Now let's consider how we can improve at the next step.

SERVICE POINT 2: SALON ENTRY

As the saying goes, "There's no second chance to make a first impression." A person's entry into the salon tells him or her many things. B. F. Skinner, the famed Harvard University professor and founder of the School of Behavioristic Psychology, showed clearly how important reinforcement is (rewarding a person when he exhibits desirable behavior). Certainly a client's entry into a salon is desirable behavior for that salon and needs to be reinforced by a staff member's attention.

Skinner's experiments showed that what was reinforced tended to occur again if reinforcement occurred immediately after the desirable action.

To enhance its chances of having a client return, the salon needs to reinforce that client's entry. In other words, it is important for people to feel welcome, recognized, and important at this service point. It is also vital that the client feel "good vibes" from the total salon environment.

Let's observe the differences between 1.0 and 5.0 service ratings:

1.0 Salon Service	5.0 Salon Service
No one to greet client at entry, or client ignored.	Client immediately acknowledged, cheerful welcome.
No directions given; client feels anxiety about how to act and what to do.	Client is invited to reception area, assisted with coat, and offered reassurance.
Client senses cold "people atmosphere," tension among staff.	Warm smiles, friendly attitudes, and harmony in salon help client relax.
Upon entry, client immediately senses cold physical environment without High-Touch ambiance.	Upon entry client sees attractive salon colors; cleanliness, music, staff appearance suggest warm High-Touch as well as High-Tech physical environment.
Client is responsible for making herself at home.	Salon staff takes responsibility to help this "stranger" become a "comfortable friend."

Add any suggestions of your own to provide better service at the point where the client enters the salon:

_____

_____

_____

_____

_____

SERVICE POINT 3: SALON RECEPTION AREA AND PRE-SERVICE EXPERIENCES

The salon's most underestimated area of potential for service is the reception area. A client waits — often bored, with little to do — stares at the walls, looks at other people, or reads a magazine. Some salons have been studying this area to help people spend this time usefully. Perhaps clients could learn more about the salon — pictures, biographies, or styles done by its professional staff — and the benefits the salon has to offer.

It is true that most delays are the fault of clients who are late; nevertheless, dealing with the waiting time of punctual clients is the salon's responsibility. When it is obvious that a certain stylist is running significantly late, it is often salon policy to call the following clients and inform them of the delay. Most people have things they would rather do than wait in the reception area.

Let's contrast the 1.0 and the 5.0 salons in their ways of approaching service in the reception area:

1.0 Salon Service

Client just waits.

5.0 Salon Service

The nail technician or skin-care specialist takes a few minutes to show the client how to care for skin or nails. Client sees additional services salon offers.

Client just waits.	A stylist who is free at the time takes a few minutes to share some ideas about home hair-care products or other services of the salon.
Client just waits.	Client watches videos related to hairstyle and lifestyle.
Client just waits.	Salon gives client brochure on the relationship between appearance and success on the job, appearance and popularity.
Client just waits — another one joins in the wait.	Receptionist shares with the client the salon's new promotion program giving a free cut for every two clients she refers.
Clients just wait, occasionally glancing at each other.	Receptionist starts to excite the client by telling her about the special skills her stylist has, e.g., perming. Asks client, "Have you ever had a perm? I'd think you'd look great!"
Clients form Salon Client Waiters' Club.	A free hair-color consultation is given to the client.
Client leaves waiting area to get his/her service.	Client leaves reception area inquiring if it is possible to get both color and a perm in the same appointment and if the salon's client-referral program can be used more than once.

Client forgotten about.

Client receives letter from salon during week with staff apologies for the delay. Salon knows she is a busy woman. Referral system's rules changed only for her — one for one!

Add some thoughts and suggestions of your own on how to reach 5.0 salon service in the reception and pre-service areas:

_____

_____

_____

_____

_____

SERVICE POINT 4: CONSULTATION

The professional cosmetologist or barber/stylist is an expert in hair cutting, coloring, perming, home care, and everything else that relates to the cosmetic improvement of the client. The study of Salon Psychology assists the professional stylist in communicating more effectively with clients through empathy and the other skills we address in this book. You will be studying about the importance of a client's self-image, both inner and outer. Everything points to one fact: A cosmetologist, especially one who has taken time to study people, is in an excellent position to serve as a consultant of hair, image, and matching hairstyle to client's lifestyle.

From our perspective, the best time for the service point of consultation to occur is prior to the shampooing. The reason is this: The stylist is seeing the client in a natural state, not with shampooed hair. And of course, the more accurate the information a stylist has about a person, the more effective her advice can be.

There is one thing that every professional stylist agrees on — consultation is a vital, necessary point of his or her work. Consultation builds client loyalty because it obviously shows that the stylist cares and is interested in providing the best possible service for clients.

GIFTS THE STYLIST AND CLIENT EACH BRING TO THE CONSULTATION

The most rewarding consultations allow both stylist and client the experience of communicating and sharing beneficial thoughts and ideas. In that special communication, both people work hard to unwrap the gift the other brings to the professional relationship.

The client's contribution to the relationship is her *LIFESTYLE*, that is, the "total person," including past experiences, present self-image, and visions of who she can be. Lifestyle comprises the total self — self as a member of a family, as part of a neighborhood, community, city, state, or society; self as part of a career, workforce, or profession; self as an earner with a certain income and financial worth; self as a spiritual member of a religion; self with certain values of life that are uncompromising; self as athletic or not; and a view of self as an attractive or unattractive person. There are no limits to the complex human being awaiting service in the stylist's chair. *WHAT A CLIENT BRINGS TO THE SALON IS A COMPLEX THING CALLED LIFESTYLE.* That is her gift to the client-stylist relationship.

Now, let's look at what the professional cosmetologist offers in meeting the *LIFESTYLE* of the client. The stylist brings a creative talent to help someone look and feel her best: skills in cutting, coloring, perming, and manicuring, and recommendations to help the client maximize her appearance. The stylist brings awareness of all of the benefits a client can receive from the salon, a knowledge of trends and new directions in hair, day-in and day-out experience in designing people's appearances. *THE STYLIST'S GIFTS TO THE RELATIONSHIP ARE KNOWLEDGE AND CREATIVITY FOR THE CLIENT'S MAXIMUM BENEFIT.*

The difference between 1.0 salon service and 5.0 salon service at Service Point 4 is simply this: The 5.0 salon *HAS A PLAN* and offers consultation initiated by the stylist with every client, except in the case of standing weekly appointments.

Contrast the 1.0, the 3.0, and the 5.0 salon on consultation:

1.0 Salon Service	**3.0 Salon Service**	**5.0 Salon Service**
No consultation.	Consultation given when requested.	Consultation offered to every client.

Add suggestions or thoughts that you have to improve service at the consultation service point:

_____

_____

_____

_____

SERVICE POINT 5: SHAMPOOING

When a client moves from the consultation area to the shampooing area, is she accompanied by someone and properly introduced at the next service point or is she simply told to go there?

Let's contrast the 1.0 and 5.0 salon in terms of their service attitude toward the client in the shampooing area:

1.0 Salon Service	**5.0 Salon Service**
No psychological contact before physical contact with client's hair.	Shampoo technician makes psychological contact by introduction, referring to client by name, a smile, or a handshake.

Shampoo technician provides no information about the service she is providing and believes that all she needs to do is shampoo hair.

Shampoo technician sees self as an expert in hair care who has more information than the client on how to do it. Shampoo person sees herself as an educator and takes pride in product knowledge. Shows client step-by-step ways to care for her own hair.

Shampoo technician takes personal calls on client's time.

Salon professional, sensitive to service and client's needs, shows respect by telling receptionist, "I can't take that call now; I'm with Mrs. G."

Shampoo technician inconsiderate of client by not being concerned about the client's comfort.

Person shampooing hair seeks feedback on water temperature and is sensitive to pressure applied during manipulation.

Shampoo technician sees self as isolated from the other stylists. Does not work as part of the team.

Shampoo technician sees self as a member of a team and helps client feel excited about going to the next service point, the styling area.

Add any suggestions in order to service a client more sensitively in the shampoo area:

_____

_____

_____

_____

_____

SERVICE POINT 6: TECHNICAL SERVICES AND RECOMMENDATIONS

The actual technical service is the meat of the whole salon experience. As dinner is the reason one goes to a restaurant, cut, color, or perm is the reason a client goes to a salon. The other service points are not the dinner, but they are the background music that makes dinner more enjoyable: the candle on the table to bring the right atmosphere, the bottle of champagne, the friendly waitress, the chef who comes to your table. You can go to a restaurant and have "something to eat," or you can have "a dining experience" designed around your own needs to relax and feel comfortable, recognized, and important. All indicators are that the average person will pay more for that.

The 5.0 service salon spends time carefully assessing the client's expectations and clarifying them to make sure they are shared and mutually agreed upon. The excellent salon has stylists who are sensitive to body language, especially facial expressions, at every step of the process. In cases where the client is experiencing new services, the ultimate salon makes sure its professionals reassure her if she is unaware of how the procedures work. The winning salon respects and doesn't intimidate clients or discourage questions. It realizes full well that the average person hasn't taken 1,500 or 2,000 hours in beauty school.

Contrast the difference between the 1.0 and 5.0 salon and stylist during the technical service point:

1.0 Salon Service	**5.0 Salon Service**
Lack of attention to client. Continually walks away.	Immersed in service. Shows client she is special; refuses phone calls of a personal nature.
Just gives service without explaining.	Shares with client what she is doing from time to time. Sensitive to client's anxieties, uncertainties. Takes the mystery out of the process.

Apathetic to client inconveniences.	Sensitive to client comfort, e.g., avoids dripping perm solution, itching cut hair on neck, color stains on skin.
Client not informed when service finished; feels stupid about salon etiquette.	Good-communicating stylist escorts client to the next service point.

Add your suggestions to improve technical services or recommendations in the salon:

_____

_____

_____

_____

SERVICE POINT 7: CLIENT REACTION AND FEEDBACK FROM SERVICES

The stylist pulled the cape off the client's shoulders, glanced briefly at her, and asked "What do you think?" and, without waiting for an answer, looked for the next client. The client experienced a stylist who wasn't honestly interested in what she really thought. The stylist was functioning on automatic pilot as it is so easy to do under the demands and stresses of the average day in a busy salon. The client is more aware of the treatment than the stylist is.

It's easy to ask for client reactions to services: The hard part is to really listen! The High-Touch, confident stylist takes negative feedback as a learning opportunity because it allows her to correct any problems and thus improve. Stylists who encourage feedback, especially from dissatisfied people, are in touch with what research has found.

Studies demonstrate the importance of creating an atmosphere where people feel safe and are encouraged to voice their dissatisfaction. The Technical Assistance Research Program commissioned by the Carter Administration spoke about the importance of service. Among their findings on handling dissatisfied customers and creating systems to get feedback are the following:

- The average business never hears from ninety-six percent of its unhappy customers. For every complaint received, the average is in fact twenty-six customers with problems, six of which are "serious" problems.

- Complainers are more likely than noncomplainers to do business again with the company that upset them, even if the problem isn't satisfactorily resolved.

- Of the customers who register complaints, between fifty-four and seventy percent will do business again with the organization if their complaints are resolved. That figure goes up to a staggering ninety-five percent if customers feel that the complaints were resolved quickly.

- The average customer who has a problem with an organization tells nine or ten people about it. Thirteen percent of people who have a problem with an organization recount the incident to more than twenty people.

- Customers who have complained to an organization and had their complaints satisfactorily resolved tell an average of five people about the treatment they received.

What does all this tell the service-oriented salon? First, just because someone doesn't tell the salon that she was dissatisfied, doesn't mean she was satisfied, because ninety-six percent never share their complaints. Second, a salon needs to have a sensitive system that encourages a dissatisfied person to feel comfortable discussing her concern. Third, the salon can keep that client by making every effort to assuage her dissatisfaction. Fourth, the business value of one client is in that client's word-of-mouth effect on the salon. Seek out, find, and service the dissatisfied client. Success is yours!

The 5.0 salon service team knows the facts that lie deep within this research. Success or failure today depends upon three things: satisfying people's wants and needs, creating a system by which they can feel safe to share their feelings, and responding to their feedback.

The 1.0 salon doesn't encourage feedback and client reaction, either out of inflated ego or lack of confidence (which underneath are the same), or doesn't really listen to client feedback. In either case it ignores the facts, the research, and sadly . . . its own future.

OPPORTUNITY IS KNOCKING FOR A STYLIST WHO DOESN'T INTIMIDATE

I have never seen a greater time of opportunity for any salon than today — that is, for a people-oriented salon. Last year while I was on some call-in radio and TV talk shows, almost every caller expressed the same concern about feeling afraid or intimidated by her stylist. In most cases he or she chose to leave that stylist and find a more service-oriented one.

This is a time of prosperity for any stylist who has the courage to seek out honest reactions from people at this seventh and very important service point in the salon experience.

1.0 Salon Service
Doesn't ask how client likes the service.

5.0 Salon Service
Realizes that the most important reason the client comes is to look and feel better, and finding out if the client is satisfied is the vital question.

Add any additional suggestions to improve the client's willingness to be honest and share his or her reactions to the technical services:

_____

_____

_____

_____

SERVICE POINT 8:
REMUNERATION FOR SERVICES

Roget's Thesaurus equates remuneration with "reward." The client's paying for the services she receives in the salon is the reward the salon owner gets for establishing a business and the staff gets for providing service.

Some stylists are almost apologetic or defensive about asking a client for payment. These stylists forget that the service they have to offer is one by which they help a client look and feel good. They should be proud to be rewarded for fine service. Why?

It's very simple. For the client's sake. A client who has been extremely satisfied by excellent service in a 5.0 salon wants to see that salon stay in business. She wants her stylist to stay successful so she can in the future continue to have her wants and needs satisfied. For that salon to remain in business, there must be a payment. (If a salon is a 1.0 salon and isn't service oriented, do you think a client would have the same attitude toward it?)

Notice the difference between 1.0 salon service and 5.0 salon service at the remuneration service point:

1.0 Salon Service	5.0 Salon Service
Hands client the check and allows her to return to the reception area alone to wait for someone to take her money.	Escorts client to the reception area where the stylist/receptionist reassures her that she made the right decision.
Allows client to leave salon without recommending proper home hair-care maintenance.	Makes sure that proper home hair-care products are recommended so client can get the most out of her investment.
Works on a "cash only" basis.	Makes many different modes of payment available to client.

Asks client to pay up front so that the receptionist may leave early.

Receptionist stays in salon until the last client has left.

Add your suggestions to provide better service at the remuneration service point:

_____

_____

_____

_____

_____

SERVICE POINT 9:
STAFF-SUPPORTED CLIENT DEBUT

We talked about the power of first impressions, but there is also the power of last impressions — Service Point 9 — in which the salon shows its interest and continued support of the client as she makes her debut with her new style, perm, or color. In the cases where the client has had the courage to change styles, it is especially important that the salon support her decision and communicate its further support for her until the next appointment. She must know the staff is behind her.

Contrast the difference between 1.0 salon support and 5.0 salon support:

1.0 Salon Support
Allows client to depart without any comment on her appearance, leaving client with the feeling, "Why did I spend the extra money if the salon didn't even see the difference."

5.0 Salon Support
Compliments some aspect of the client's hair, skin, or nails.

Salon staff assumes client has the tools, the skills, and the knowledge to care for hair at home.	Salon professional further reinforces the client's need for home hair-care enhancement support by recommending the best tools, products, and knowledge to care for hair (if stylist forgot).
Staff allows client to leave without a plan for continuing the relationship.	Salon shows support and interest in the client by scheduling the next appointment. Salon calls client in the interim if client either seemed a little uncertain during the feedback service or received a new service.

In a 5.0 salon-supported client debut, the client feels new-found confidence in her relationship with a service-oriented salon of professional cosmetologists who stand beside her and support her needs. That is the ultimate in service! The salon has given her a guarantee of a long-term relationship, which means she doesn't have to go through the consultation process again somewhere else, with someone she doesn't know. Her search is over! That's something a 1.0 salon service just wouldn't do.

Add any suggestions you can for providing sensitive ways to help clients feel supported by your salon team members when clients debut with a new style:

_____

_____

_____

_____

_____

Congratulations! You have just experienced one of the most rigorous service-sensitive training programs for salon professionals. At times you may have been overwhelmed with how complex doing a "good job" seems. But it's actually not. You see, each of the points in this chapter reflects the ideal, not the typical. There are very few, if any, salons in the world that are totally and completely 5.0 all the time, good days and bad. These ideas are designed to get you thinking about a plan for providing better service.

IF YOU TOOK JUST ONE IDEA AND PUT IT TO USE IN YOUR SALON TODAY, YOU HAVE GROWN!

You now know: The difference between success and failure is SERVICE!

A SALON'S SERVICE CAN BE MEASURED. Salon's service attitudes range from negative (1.0) to mediocre (3.0) to positive and excellent (5.0). The difference in the rating of a salon's service attitude is seen in whether the *SALON HAS A SERVICE PLAN AND LIVES UP TO ITS SERVICE PLAN AT THE KEY SERVICE POINTS IN THE SALON!*

CHAPTER 4

VIBRATING WITH AN OPTIMISTIC, UPBEAT ATTITUDE!

You have related to your client with 5.0 High-Touch Empathy and 5.0 High-Tech Design and have created a 5.0 service attitude with a plan at all key points. What about you? How can you keep yourself motivated and going?

DO YOU WANT TO LIMIT THE VISION OF WHO YOU CAN BE IN THE FUTURE BASED UPON WHO YOU WERE IN THE PAST?

or

DO YOU WANT TO CREATE YOUR FUTURE?

DO YOU WANT TOMORROW TO BE BETTER THAN YESTERDAY?

It can be if you convey a 5.0 optimistic, upbeat attitude!

Soon You Will Be Able To:

- Recognize the advantages of being an "UP" person.

- Become an "UP" person by doing all of the things that "UP" people do.

- Take charge of your life rather than have your life take charge of you.

THE ON-THE-WAY-UP ATTITUDE!

A few years ago while spending a week in Perth, Western Australia, I had an opportunity to observe the difference between up people and down people. I ate breakfast at my hotel every day for a week and began to see something that opened my eyes to the role of attitude — not luck — in success!

The waitress who served me the first day, let's call her Jane, had a down disposition. She was down on people, down on the manager, and down on the hotel. She hated tourists and said to me, "No offense, but Americans are arrogant!"

Serving the other side of the restaurant was a charming, smiling girl with a cheeriness that brightened everyone's outlook. Even though Margaret was not serving my table, she came over to warm up my coffee with a bouncy, "How are you today, sir? If there's any way we can make this a better day for you, we'd love to!"

By the third day, I started to notice something quite interesting as I waited in line to be seated. Customers were asking if they could go to Margaret's section. In fact, one couple actually waited to have breakfast just to be with Margaret!

Interested in studying UP people, I decided that before the week ended, I was going to find out why Margaret differed from Jane. From outside appearances, they were about equally attractive. Certainly Margaret was earning more money than Jane because of having more customers and bigger tips per customer. Was Margaret the product of good, positive experiences in life and Jane the product of hard times?

On my last morning in Perth, I spent an eye-opening fifteen minutes trying to learn some answers to explain this success story. I asked Margaret if she was married. She said yes, but she hadn't seen her husband in more than five years. They loved each other very dearly but had shared a life experience that lasted only a few moments before they were separated forever. The couple attempted to escape from behind the Iron Curtain to go to Australia. She made it but he didn't. She had been unsuccessful in reaching him; he had no idea where she was, and she couldn't ever go back to see the man she loved and had married! And this was the waitress whose UP attitude was lifting everyone else's spirits!

That day the hairdressers of Western Australia received one of the most inspiring talks I ever gave — because I was inspired by someone who showed me the human ability to rise UP and above and create a new attitude. Both UP and down people are going places — but they are going in different directions!

FACTS ON UPBEAT PEOPLE!

We will soon be seeing how the 1.0 down person looks at life differently and acts differently from the 5.0 UP PERSON. But first here are a few facts about the effects of a person's attitude on that person's life.

Fact #1: *UP PEOPLE,* when ill, recuperate faster than down people.

Fact #2: *UP PEOPLE* have better social relationships and more friends than down people.

Fact #3: *UP PEOPLE* experience fewer depressions than down people.

Fact #4: *UP PEOPLE* enjoy their work more than down people.

Fact #5: Although it's not yet conclusive, evidence is strong to support the fact that *UP PEOPLE* live longer.

There is no downside risk to being positive!

Choose the UP way: It's the way UP.

Attitude is everything. Earl Nightingale in his book, *Earl Nightingale's Greatest Discovery*, writes, "To ask, 'What is the role of attitude in a person's success or failure?' is much like asking, 'What is the role of granite in the Himalayas?' or 'What is the role of H$_2$O in the Pacific Ocean?' Attitude comes very close to being everything about success or failure. With a great attitude, a person can succeed though he may start with very little else. Attitude makes a sale or loses it."

In the foreword to Nightingale's book, well-known author Wayne Dyer writes, "*THOUGHTS ARE THINGS.* A thought is the most powerful force in the universe. You can make of your life whatever you wish if you learn to make your thoughts work for you."

UP PEOPLE have *UP THOUGHTS*. Those *up thoughts* are the forces that drive them upward, recognizable by others in a ten-second contact.

What are the differences between the way 1.0 down people and 5.0 *UP PEOPLE* approach life?

Let's measure the differences between down and up salon professionals:

1.0 On-the-Way-Down Person	**5.0 On-the-Way-Up Person**
1. Seeks advice from losers or people who will support his attitude on being down on life. Asks people who have either failed or haven't tried to achieve a task if the task is possible. They say, "No, don't waste your time." Down person gives up, sees successful people achieve the task, and claims they were lucky or got the break.	1. Seeks out advice from winners, achievers, and successes — other UP PEOPLE! Having achieved these accomplishments themselves, they give the advice, "Sure you can do it." The UP PERSON is inspired, and this energy and motivation spur him onward to "find a way." (In some cases, an UP PERSON will even take a trip to spend

a few moments with someone who is a top achiever in his field of interest.) Goes to lectures by UP PEOPLE. Finds consultants who are believers in overcoming the impossible. Reads success books by people who overcame barriers and reached the top. (At this point, just compare the differences between the 1.0 and 5.0 person as to where each seeks sources of advice. You will begin to see how each person's approach, plugging into positive or negative sources, determines what he becomes.)

2. Finds excuses, looks for things or people to blame for being held back. "Why wasn't I born into money?"

2. Sees excuses for what they are — using energies to build a case explaining why he couldn't do it — instead of using energies to DO IT. When told by someone that you can't really get ahead if you're not born into money, explains, "Since 1928 only two presidents of the United States were born into money, and president of the U.S. is one of the most powerful positions in the world."

3. Arrives at work down, drags everyone else down, feels persecuted by life.

3. Is a stimulant, a lifter to everyone at work. Everyone likes to be around this positive energy force who is missed when not in the salon.

4. Every day is the same. Same clothing, same haircut, same ideas on life. Dull, boring, negative.

4. Fresh, exciting, and creative. Brings new looks and new ideas, is unpredictable. Takes a boring job and makes a game of it. Sends cards or writes letters to other people even when there isn't a birthday or any other event.

5. Takes credit for everything.

5. Gives credit to everyone; never takes credit.

6. Sees others in the salon as competition.

6. Sees others in the salon team as equals; cooperates and encourages others. Is a positive and constructive force in the salon environment.

7. Backbiter; always eager to talk about people behind their backs.

7. Is always up-front with people. If necessary can be assertive and deal with issues. Turns gossipy, backbiting conversations into constructive, pick-up ones. This person is, over the long haul, the most trusted friend of everyone in the salon.

8. Makes it unfashionable for others to say they actually enjoy hairstyling. Puts these people down as "squares."

9. Gives orders to everyone.

10. Sees what's wrong with everything, but doesn't attempt to change anything.

11. Sees problems.

12. Has to be constantly told what to do, not a self-starter. Has to be told to attend educational shows or in-salon programs.

13. Late; holds an irresponsible attitude toward professional responsibilities.

14. Sees only one point of view (selfish) and doesn't believe in the importance of a salon team feeling.

8. Proud to be part of the hairstyling profession and builds pride in others, especially those who go the extra mile for the client or the other professionals in the salon.

9. Gives life and energy to others.

10. Sees what's right with others. Always starts off conversations with a compliment.

11. Sees challenges and solutions.

12. Self-igniting, responsible, anticipates problems ahead of time and has a plan to prevent things from getting worse. Seeks out educational programs; takes pride in learning new styles, perms, and colors.

13. Ethical, understands professional responsibilities to clients, coworkers, and salon.

14. Considerate of others and always tries to see the other side of the story in a disagreement. Salon professionals often turn to this person for help in solving conflicts between people.

15. Speaks in a *DOWN* vocabulary:	15. Speaks with an *UPBEAT* vocabulary!
Things are awful, terrible.	We face an exciting challenge here in the salon.
I hate aging.	I enjoy the opportunity of growing and maturing. After all, what are the alternatives to aging?
I'm too old to change.	My experiences give me an opportunity to change. The world is changing; my profession is changing. To stay in tune, I will not only change but enjoy the excitement of it.
I'm too young to do that.	Achievement doesn't discriminate against youth. Anyway, the biggest and most important part of trying something new is not in the achievement but in the learning one gets from the attempt. In my youth I can explore new things and can learn each time.
Maybe it can be done.	It absolutely *CAN BE DONE* — and we here in the salon are made of the stuff that can do it. Let's get started.
Let's give up. It's no use.	Let's put ourselves into second gear and Find a Way.

UP PEOPLE are stimulants, magnets who attract others around them. The responsible, *UPBEAT* salon professional experiences many social, financial, physical, spiritual, and personal benefits that the down person doesn't. Being *UP* isn't the result of being born in the right home or of getting the breaks in life. It is a personal choice.

VIBRATE WITH AN OPTIMISTIC, UPBEAT ATTITUDE!

CHAPTER 5

CREATIVELY FILLING UP YOUR BOOK

Styling with High-Touch Empathy and High-Tech Crafts-
manship, coupled with sensitive service and upbeat attitude,
guarantees you success. You will keep your clients and add
many more with creative ways of filling up your book.

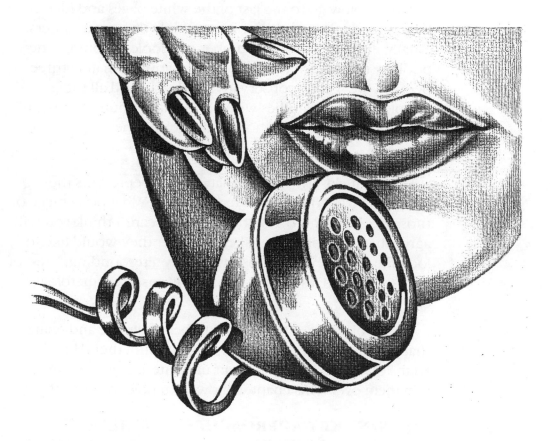

Soon You Will Be Able To:

- Experience the long-term pride of keeping the clients who now come to you.

- Feel the thrill of building your future by getting new clients from existing ones.

- Build your clientele by using your creative mind rather than waiting for people to arrive from "clientland."

OPEN YOUR MIND TO THE CEILINGLESS SKY OF POTENTIAL

Take just a few minutes of your life to really experience this exercise: Find a telephone book and go to the first page where names are listed. Count the number of names on just one page. Now go to the last of the white pages and identify that page number. At this point, multiply the two numbers. Finally, multiply this total number of people in your phone book by three (each name represents approximately three people). We will be conservative and disregard all those people and their families who have unlisted numbers as well as all those who choose not to have telephones.

Now write down your total number: _____

Look at it closely because that number represents the people who need what you have to offer. What percentage of those people want to look the best they can? I think you will agree that if people were asked whether they would like to look the best they can, most would say a resounding, "Yes, of course!" And that's the gift you, as a licensed cosmetologist, can give.

Now look again at that total number of people and realize that you have what they need — if you fulfill their High-Tech/High-Touch needs and use your unlimited, creative mind to win them over. This chapter shows you how to do that!

THE NINE KEY APPROACHES TO BUILDING YOUR FUTURE BY BUILDING YOUR CLIENTELE

1. Make a commitment to retain every client you currently service.

2. Use your current clients as referral sources for future clients.

3. Ask advice of stylists who are talented at building clientele.

4. Expand your client-appeal base by relating to a variety of different age ranges and cultural backgrounds.

5. Associate and network with other professional, occupational, and career groups.

6. Create opportunities to give yourself greater community exposure.

7. Compliment people's hair wherever you go.

8. Seek out and invite high-profile and respected members of the community into your salon.

9. Advertise the benefits of coming to your salon.

Future Builder #1:

MAKE A COMMITMENT TO RETAIN EVERY CLIENT YOU CURRENTLY SERVICE!

If you want to guarantee an increase in clients this year, the surest way to make that happen is not to lose any clients you currently serve. Some stylists who start to build up a book make the mistake of taking existing clients for granted. And frequently a veteran client will hear from a friend about a good experience she had at another salon. When your client gives the new salon a try, she is greeted with enthusiasm and enjoys all the attention. Just as personal relationships sometimes get stale after a while and need to be refreshed, so it is with the stylist-client relationship.

Retaining current clients is of prime importance. As you read through this textbook, you might take note that most of the study of Salon Psychology relates to keeping clients by satisfying their needs. Here are a few tips to help you do this.

1. Send a card, not only for a birthday or special occasion, but any time. Just as Stevie Wonder sang in his popular song, "I Just Called to Say 'I Love You,'" you might send a card that suggests, "I just wrote to say 'Thank you.'" Joe Girard, the greatest automobile salesman in the world, makes it a practice to send out more than 13,000 thank-you cards every single month, for many different reasons. What a thrill it is to receive a card with a positive thought from a person who serves you professionally. Start with those who have been coming to you the longest, and prove to them you aren't taking them for granted. Then watch how people come in to tell you how much they appreciated your note!

2. Build relationships faster with new clients by finding commonalties you share with them. "Oh, you have a two-year-old also. Aren't they something?" "Yes, Mrs. Smith, my husband and I also enjoy vacationing in Florida. Have you ever been to Disney World?" Or, "Yes, we were out at the ballpark last week. You love baseball, too?"

3. Try to remember previous conversations and especially remember things that are important to your clients. "How is your little dog Bogart?" Some stylists have even found this point important enough that they take three-by-five file cards and in less than a half minute jot down something important in the client's life or an upcoming event she's looking forward to. Does she open her eyes wide when she comes to the chair six weeks later and the stylist comments, "How did your dinner turn out for your in-laws?" Rapport is immediately reestablished. High Touch!

4. Listen for a person's claims to fame. Claims to fame are the proud moments of achievement in people's lives. "You really won the outstanding golfer of the year award? Oh, that must have been a great feeling!" Or, "Isn't it tough to supervise a whole sales force from all over the country?" "So, you're a pretty good dancer,

Stacey? And only seven years old. Wow!" When you show interest in someone's claims, you turn her on and she feels important in your presence — a sure way to keep a client.

5. Compliment people's dress, appearance, or children.

6. Make every person you touch feel important, special, and unique.

7. Be a good-news giver, a stimulant, an upper!

Remember, when you lose one person, you then have to get two more in order to keep your future building. Have a plan today to retain every existing client.

Add some ideas of your own:

_____

_____

_____

_____

_____

Future Builder #2:

USE YOUR CURRENT CLIENTS AS REFERRAL SOURCES FOR FUTURE CLIENTS

When you go to your family doctor, you probably don't give any thought to the idea, "If I'm treated well, I will tell others about my good experience and will encourage them to go to the same doctor." Yet if the doctor provided excellent and competent diagnosis and treatment coupled with good High-Touch service and asked if you would please tell your friends about him or her, chances are a name or two would flash through your mind. But if the doctor never asked you, chances are you wouldn't think of it. That's how important it is to make it known that you are looking for clients and to show your appreciation for the help your clients can give. Believe it or not, they do want to help you!

Word-of-mouth referrals are the most effective, and it's easy to understand why. It is probable that the clients currently coming to you like your work and personality. Out of all the potential stylists they could choose, they selected you. The friends, relatives, and coworkers of these clients trust their opinions more than they would trust a series of multimillion-dollar ads on television or anything that the yellow pages might say about your salon. All you have to do is make it known to your satisfied clients that you would like their help in finding future clients to make happy.

Here are a few ideas on how to get your message across:

1. Have signs posted throughout the salon that encourage clients to be a helpful referral source. "If you really like your style, color, or perm and the way you were treated today, please tell your friends. We would really appreciate it."

2. Thank your clients in advance for sending in others.

3. Talk to them about people. "Oh, your friend Debbie, whom you talk about — does she need a stylist? I'd love to meet her!"

4. Give people added incentives to stimulate referrals from among their friends. "Bring a friend in, and I'll style both of you for the cost of one!"

5. Create a Board of Advisers from your best clients, and give them free products and services for help in generating creative suggestions for increasing salon clientele. They love contributing their ideas.

Add some ideas of your own to get future clients from your existing ones:

_____

_____

_____

_____

_____

Remember, give your current clients good High-Tech/High-Touch service, and encourage them to think of one other person who might also benefit from your services. Theoretically, you could double your clientele at no cost to you!

Future Builder #3:

ASK ADVICE OF STYLISTS WHO ARE TALENTED AT BUILDING CLIENTELE

It is an interesting fact that the best people in any profession — the real professionals — are the ones most willing to share their ideas with others. They are complimented when people ask them for help. And you remind them of themselves because they can identify with your drive.

Choose a few stylists, owners, or managers whom you respect and who have a good following. Compliment them and show your respect. Ask if they would be kind enough to help you get started. Then listen carefully, thank them, and give them a little gift, like a heartfelt letter, a card, flowers, or dinner. Praise them in front of their clients.

As they share ideas with you, watch their eyes open wide and their arms fly enthusiastically, telling how they did it. Watch how they return to keep helping you develop your future. And when you successfully use ideas people have given you, share the good news with them, by all means. Always, always give them credit for their help.

Add some other ways that you could approach a successful stylist for advice:

_____

_____

_____

_____

_____

_____

Future Builder #4:

EXPAND YOUR CLIENT-APPEAL BASE BY RELATING TO A VARIETY OF DIFFERENT AGE RANGES AND CULTURAL BACKGROUNDS

While stylists tend to deal with all age ranges, most feel especially comfortable within certain limits. The most common comfort zone for stylists seems to be in their own age group. Some sensitive stylists are aware of this and recognize that after a period of time they seem to attract clients around their own ages. This is understandable because a stylist's manner and dress seem to attract people of similar taste, further proof, of course, of the importance of psychology and High-Touch relating.

As one stylist from Brisbane, Australia, observed, "I've been in the business for sixteen years, and I just started to notice that my clients are getting a lot older over the years. They were much younger when I got started. Some of the younger guys in the salon, with their snappy dress, are getting the younger clients. Then I thought, 'Why wouldn't the clients go to Phil and Dave? They relate to them much more than to an old-timer like me.' So I started to listen to what they talk about, the music they listen to. I'm even dressing a little differently. You know what? At first it was a little uncomfortable, but now I feel I can relate to the younger clients better. And I know I am keeping more of my younger walk-ins."

On the other side of the age range, a young stylist who had just started working in a New Jersey salon with a disproportionate number of senior-citizen clientele felt very uneasy with them. But Brenda was open-minded enough to listen. She soon learned a lot about the important things in their world. She, herself, grew from their experiences, which they loved to share with her. Brenda even commented that when she visited her grandmother in Michigan, they got along a lot better!

In this area, as the case of the Brisbane stylist shows, you can expand clientele and build the future by being open to serving age ranges beyond the narrow span of your own.

A stylist can benefit, as well, by understanding other cultures and experiences. If you want to live and work in Florida, especially in Miami, it would be wise to learn more about the Puerto Rican or Cuban cultures and even to learn Spanish. Some stylists limit their base by not learning about clients of other religions, nationalities, and, in some cases, the opposite sex.

The more open the mind, the more willing to learn about other age ranges and other cultures, the larger a pool of clients one can attract. Think about that phone book again!

Future Builder #5:

ASSOCIATE AND NETWORK WITH OTHER PROFESSIONAL, OCCUPATIONAL, AND CAREER GROUPS

Popularity of the Rotary, Kiwanis, and other clubs is due not only to social reasons but to business reasons as well. These clubs provide an opportunity to support each other through networking. Two years ago I had an opportunity to speak to a women's networking group of more than three hundred in Winnipeg, Manitoba. What struck me was the enthusiasm they felt for each other, even though their professions, occupations, and careers varied so widely — from dentists to hairstylists to real estate agents to teachers. It was beautiful to observe the camaraderie and support they shared. Indeed, networking is the wave of the future.

In *Megatrends*, John Naisbitt calls networking "people talking to each other, sharing ideas, information, and resources." He adds, "Networks exist to foster self-help, to exchange information, to change society, to improve productivity and worklife, and to share resources. They are structured to transmit information in a way that is quicker, more High Touch, and more energy efficient than any other process we know."

With so many daily contacts from many kinds of careers, the hairstylist is in an ideal position to create a networking group. She can contribute her expertise in fashionable hair care while other groups bring their special knowledge. A social hour with shared knowledge and resources adds up to everyone's benefit.

There is another benefit. In observing stylists who burn out faster than others, one thing became obvious to me. Those who burn out tend to associate with hairstylists after work and talk about the same things at night as they did during the day. Turned-on stylists are likely to have a rich variety of friends and interests from all walks of life. So not only is networking good for building clientele, but it is also good for building your own quality of life.

As a licensed cosmetologist, you have much to give others in the important area of appearance. Travel through the phone book's yellow pages and open up your mind as you observe all of the different businesses, professions, careers, and occupations. In each instance, ask yourself these two questions:

1. What do I have or what can I do to help them? and

2. What do they have that can help me?

For example, how could I network with a psychologist who has a private practice?

Idea #1: I have a lot of clients who have problems that they share with me, many with serious emotional problems who don't know where to turn. So I can ask the psychologist if I could refer clients to him or her.

Idea #2: The psychologist works with people's inner image, and often when people begin to grow through therapy, they also start to take better care of their appearance. I could give the psychologist my card and ask if he or she would keep me in mind for referring clients, because people feel great after a perm, color, or cut. The psychologist and I could become a mutual networking system, to each other's and the client's benefit.

Take a few days to think about the following list of different groups. When you meet someone who describes his or her profession, you should be able immediately to see a network connection with him or her.

Profession	Some Possible Network Connection
Advertisers	Design free ads in return for free haircuts?
Airlines	Flight attendants special rates?
Antique Dealers	Hairstyles from the era of his/her historical specialty?
Attorneys	Style the hair of the defendant?
Automobile Dealers	Showrooms are important: The "showroom" of their sales force is their appearance.
"Balloons for Special Occasions"	Why not?
Bridal Shops	WOW!
Businesses	YES!
Charitable Organizations	Special cut-a-thons for a cause?
Chauffeur Service	Appearance a must!
Churches	Hundreds and hundreds of them.
Communications Consultants	What does your appearance communicate?
Employment and Personnel Agencies	WOW!
Florists	WOW!
Formal Wear	YES!

Let your mind creatively flow.

Fraternal Organizations	American Legion, VFW.
Funeral Directors	Think about it!
Health Clubs	Unlimited opportunities.
Health and Diet-Food Stores	YES!

Holistic Practitioners	You give people the natural look.
Hospitals	Administrators, specials for nurses, LPNs?
Hotels	So much potential here, you could make a living with their employees!
Jewelers	One Media, Pennsylvania, jeweler allows a skin-care specialist to wear any piece of jewelry free for the day because he knows people will ask, "Where did you get that?"
Language Schools	A French or Oriental look? YOU CAN DO IT!
Magicians	Don't laugh!
Marriage Counselors	If the couple's problem is one of appearance . . .
Men's Clothing	Imagine a poorly groomed salesman.
Musicians	In the public's eye.
Painters	They are interested in color, too!
Photo Finishing	Think about it!
Photographers	They want their pictures to turn out well.
Real Estate Agents	Network by referring clients who tell you they are thinking about moving from an apartment to a home, and to you the agents refer clients who move into town.
Restaurant Employees	High-exposure people — "Who did your hair?"
Schools	Schools don't feel proud of poorly groomed students.
Secretarial Services	Are you kidding?
Tax Consultants	Not a bad idea!

Vitamin and Food Supplements	The healthy look.
Welcoming Services for Newcomers	YES!
Women's Apparel	Obvious by now, isn't it?

These are just for starters. Some groups will be easy to network with, others a little more difficult. Remember to ask yourself the two questions of what can I give them and what can they give me, and let your creative mind flow, building a network and building your future!

You can also market your services by targeting a specific profession or business. What if you developed a simple brochure which described the importance of first impressions and appearance on sales and went to a real estate agency offering employees a special on a cut, color, or perm? Who says you can't?

Add any other of your own ideas on what you could do to build your future by networking:

_____

_____

_____

_____

_____

Future Builder #6:

CREATE OPPORTUNITIES TO GIVE YOURSELF GREATER COMMUNITY EXPOSURE

Today, more than ever before, hairstylists are tending to be more active members of their communities. It is commonplace to see stylists on local TV, hear them on the radio, or read about them in the newspaper. All of these are powerful tools not only to show the community all of the benefits people can get from a salon, but also to give the stylists exposure. This is one of the key ways of building clientele.

The most exceptional example of giving a gift to a community that I ever personally experienced was the work of a young stylist from Battle Creek, Iowa, by the name of Peggy Eason. After I spoke to salon owners in Des Moines, Peggy asked if I would consider coming to Battle Creek to talk to the people of her community on the power of being optimistic. When I asked Peggy how many people lived in Battle Creek, she informed me that there were more than eight hundred people. Not wanting her to be disappointed, I prepared her for about a dozen or so people because I know how hard it is to get people out at night. She let me know that I was surely wrong because a hairstylist touches many, many lives.

When the evening arrived, I was taken to the high school coach's office next to the gym, where my talk was to be given. At 7:30 the school superintendent knocked on the door and said, "Peggy is ready to introduce you."

As I walked out onto the gym floor expecting an audience of twenty at most, I saw every seat in the bleachers filled and people dotted around the perimeter of the gym! Standing on the gym floor in the center of all of this was my stylist friend, Peggy, holding a microphone and speaking to more than four hundred of her fellow citizens!

Through the positive efforts of one stylist, the town of Battle Creek raised monies that night for its long-desired ambulance. When people walk by the Nu Fashion Salon, they think of Peggy Eason, that special stylist who gave back to her community. A fringe benefit even though it wasn't Peggy's intent was greater exposure. Incidentally, three years later to the day, Peggy and her husband, Jay, came to a talk I was giving in Omaha, Nebraska, and added to the story. Their house had burned down, and the community of Battle Creek pulled together and nourished the family during this crisis. When you give to the community, the community gives back! Thanks, Peggy!

Here are some other suggestions to create opportunities for greater community exposure.

1. Ask the local school principals, at all levels, whether it would be possible for you to talk to students on the importance of grooming and appearance and how to take care of their hair. Classes such as home economics, health, and business fit in naturally with this plan.

2. Volunteer to participate in your local school's career day to talk about hairstyling as a career.

3. Team up with anyone conducting fashion shows and find a way to design the models' hair.

4. Local theater groups might be an ideal highway for getting good public exposure.

Add any other ideas of your own on creating opportunities to give yourself greater community exposure:

_____

_____

_____

_____

_____

Future Builder #7:

COMPLIMENT PEOPLE'S HAIR
WHEREVER YOU GO

Wherever you go, especially at parties, compliment people's hair. Envision and share with them some beautiful ways they could wear their hair, or some ideas of perm or color to match their features, clothing, etc. You will be a welcomed helper in an important area of their lives. Of course, give them your card and invite them in for a free consultation about the many, many lovely things that can be done with their hair.

Interestingly, the worse a person's hair is, the more she needs a compliment, so pick out some positive feature and compliment it. You will find her very responsive to someone who respects her hair, which means, to her, your total respect.

Keep your eyes open, and whether it be the ticket taker at the movies or the waitress at a restaurant, share a compliment and share the potential you see in her hair. Then, give a smile and your card. It works a lot better if you do it than if you don't!

Include any other thoughts you may have on places you could compliment people on their hair:

_____

_____

_____

_____

_____

Future Builder #8:

SEEK OUT AND INVITE HIGH-PROFILE AND RESPECTED MEMBERS OF THE COMMUNITY INTO YOUR SALON

A few years ago it was discovered that every social group has a leader who, when the group goes to the tavern, speaks first. "Give me a Mick!" The others tend to follow with, "I'll have the same." Advertisers picked up on this and started marketing to the high-status leader, knowing that others will follow.

You can make use of that multimillion-dollar advice by seeking out community leaders and perhaps offering them reduced-rate haircuts.

Consider some of these groups:

1. Top athletes at school, especially the team captain or leaders in achievement.

2. Cheerleaders, who have high exposure and are usually respected students.

3. Politicians.

4. Executives from local companies.

5. People whose names appear in the newspaper frequently (for positive reasons, of course).

6. TV personalities, radio disc jockeys.

Add a list of people who are your specific community leaders, and develop an incentive plan for them to become your clients:

_____

_____

_____

_____

_____

Future Builder #9:

ADVERTISE THE BENEFITS OF COMING TO YOUR SALON

This next question is so important, I'd like you to take at least a week to think it through and come up with an answer that is true, that you believe in, and that is a turn-on for potential clients.

WHAT ARE THE THREE MAIN REASONS PEOPLE SHOULD COME TO SEE YOU? LIST THREE BENEFITS THAT WILL OPEN UP THEIR EYES TO YOU:

1. _____

2. _____

3. _____

Of course you can't answer this now, but if you have jotted anything down, keep it with you and see if you can improve on it. At the end of the week, you will have the three key benefits.

You then need to advertise your key ideas along with any other relevant information about your salon. Your advertising can be yellow pages, newspapers, radio, TV, magazines, local "What's Happening in Town" booklets, theater programs, or newsletters that you do in your salon. If you get into expensive advertising, you will be gratified to know that there are co-op programs with manufacturers that can really cut down the cost. These can save you hundreds of dollars a year.

You can also do a one-page flier to pass around. To make it effective, include a special, and set a time limit. You might even want to get a few testimonials from some of your clients.

1.0 Attitude to Expanding Clientele	**5.0 Attitude to Expanding Clientele**
Those who come back, come back.	I go back to places where I feel good and so do salon clients. Those who come back do so because I make them feel good.
Who comes in, comes in.	I have many creative ways of bringing people in.

By using these nine Future Builders coupled with new ideas of your own — *FILL UP YOUR BOOK!*

CHAPTER 6

FEELING LIKE A CONTRIBUTING SALON TEAM MEMBER

You have given clients High-Tech Benefits, High-Touch Empathy, and the ultimate in salon services. You vibrate with an upbeat, optimistic attitude and have a plan to expand your clientele. Success is yours! And the opportunities for even greater success are guaranteed when you develop the final part of your professional self. That skill is your increased sensitivity to all of your co-professionals in the salon. The whole is more than the sum of its parts. This is synergy, and it is the "bonus" that is earned when good things work together for the common good. By using the ideas in this chapter, you can feel like a winning team member.

Soon You Will Be Able To:

- Grow from the little-known fact that cooperating rather than competing is a better way of reaching your goal.

- Feel better because of being part of an "us" rather than a "me."

- Get others to understand your pressure and appreciate your contributions better.

THE OPPORTUNITIES FOR TEAM PLAYERS

The 1970s were called the "Me Decade," a term coined by Tom Wolfe in a *New Yorker* magazine article. To think about self was the way to go and was "in." The me-first concept had a short life for long-term thinkers, people who began to realize that if I show that I don't think about others, in a little while they won't care about me. Consider psychiatrist Alfred Adler's assertion that the healthy, fulfilled human being is one who contributes, belongs, and adds to whatever exists at that moment. It becomes obvious that whenever someone feels something missing in himself, it is because he is retreating, not belonging, not becoming part of something greater than himself.

The '70s were the Me Decade. The '70s passed. The dress, haircuts, fashion, politics, and attitudes of that era no longer fit. The me-first feeling no longer fits. Instead of listening to the songs of the '70s, "My Way," "It's My Life," "I Gotta Be Me," and "Take This Job and Shove It," today we listen to songs like "We Are the World," "That's What Friends Are For," and other songs telling us that we as a society are growing from *me* to *we*. To be successful in our twenty-first century society, the membership fee is simply to enlist in being a *TOGETHER-WE-CAN-DO-IT* person. Isn't it nice to have allies and friends? It might be a surprise to you, but they need allies and friends too. You are one!

What completes this word, *OPPORT - - - - -?* "Unity" does: we-ness, a together-we-can-do-it feeling! There are two kinds of people in the world. One thinks that for a team or a family feeling to develop, somebody else must start it. The other person, the real success, is one who feels that no matter how small or big he is in terms of job description or income, he will take responsibility for turning any difficult situation around to help everyone. Instead of tearing down as others around him are doing, he'll build up by putting forward everybody's positive ideas. Which of these two people will be remembered as a positive contributor? We know it's the positive, contributing team player who has a view of life beyond his own narrow scene.

Any Truly Committed Team Will Defeat a Bunch of Talented Me-First Individuals.

TEAM SYNERGY IN ACTION

For 132 years the America's Cup, the ultimate prize in sailing competition, was dominated by the United States. No other country ever won it in all that time! No country even thought seriously about the possibility of having that treasured trophy in one of its own yacht clubs. Then a determined Australian, John Bertrand, realizing the Americans had the best individual yachtsmen in the world, found a way to win. In his book, *Born to Win*, Bertrand writes, "In the absence of stars, there was but one commodity we could develop, and that was team spirit. In every walk of life, a tightly grouped, determined, well-trained team will so often overcome pure genius. All they need is an explicit belief that they can fight and win, that they can overcome opposing cleverness with unshakable determination, tireless work, and a desire to back each other . . . and ultimately triumph through sheer sense of communal purpose."

The single biggest event, the most significant moment in the history of Australia that brought the Aussies together, occurred on September 26, 1983. John Bertrand and his *TEAM* of twelve yachtsmen won the America's Cup. Yes, any truly committed team will defeat a bunch of talented me-first individuals, always!

HOW CAN TEAM SYNERGY
MAKE THE DIFFERENCE IN SUCCESS?

There are a number of reasons why team power and cooperation are more effective than me-first thinking and excessive competition:

1. Team synergy helps everyone feel himself to be a contributing part of the whole. The loneliest sentence in the world is, "Nobody asked me to join in!" Team power thus satisfies each person's needs to belong and contribute.

2. Team synergy rallies a group around a common goal. It unites many individuals by giving them common interests and common achievements to celebrate.

3. Team synergy instills pride not only in oneself but also in the whole.

4. Team synergy leads to greater involvement and greater understanding of each person's role and how he fits in.

5. Team power makes cooperation and mutual encouragement the winning words of the day. Thus when faced with any situation in the salon, the team-power-oriented professional thinks, "How will this affect others?"

Let's measure the stylist's team feeling:

1.0 Self-Centered	**3.0 Average**	**5.0 Total Team Player**
Thinks "me" constantly; competes; puts others down; uninterested in cooperating; doesn't contribute positive ideas; doesn't attend meetings; drags others down.	Sometimes thinks team and the impact of her actions on others, but at other times thinks self. Not a downer, not an upper.	Thoughtful; continually supports and encourages other team members; lifts others up when down. Contributes new ideas to make the salon a better place; values the other team members and thinks, "How will my action affect others?"

THE "ME-FIRST" OR "WE" FEELING

After moving to a new city, I needed a podiatrist, checked the yellow pages, and went for foot x-rays and treatments. The x-rays did their job and saw through my feet, but I saw through the doctors. The clinic housed a bunch of individual podiatrists who couldn't care less about each other. There was no family feeling, no pictures on the wall, no unifying theme — just cold rooms, unconnected "professionals," a series of *"ME'S."*

The x-rays revealed I needed surgery, but I knew it wouldn't be at that Me-First office. If these doctors didn't care about the people they worked with every day, how could they provide proper care for me, an outsider, a mere patient they didn't even know?

Oh, I did get the surgery. This time I didn't look in the yellow pages but asked satisfied patients where to go. I heard great reviews about some other doctors who treated patients like people. As I arrived, the receptionist knew my name (pronounced Losoncy correctly), introduced me to two of the doctors when they came out to the front desk, and, believe it or not, matched me with a doctor from my home state of Pennsylvania! We both even liked the Minnesota Twins baseball team. (You don't think that High-Touch stuff is important?) I trusted this good doc to do the surgery though knowing him for fewer ticks of the clock than I knew the one who x-rayed and diagnosed my problem.

The night before I wrote this I saw all three doctors from that office, their wives, and staff out for dinner together, laughing and having fun, and, most important, they remembered my name! If this family of professionals cared about each other, in my mind they would care about me. They were "We," not "Me-First," people!

**The Whole Is More Than Just the Sum of Its Parts!
A Customer, Client, or Patient Senses the "Me-First"
or "We-Together-Can-Do-It" Feeling.**

IT CAN START WITH YOU!
CATCH THE TEAM FEELING

As one link in the chain of success improves, the whole chain gets stronger. What if all of the links improve and become the best links each can? Then the chain becomes as strong as it is possible to be.

The receptionist's success depends upon the growth, attitude, and skills of the combined team of owner, manager, stylist, specialist, shampoo technician, and everyone else. The stylist's success depends upon the very same things. And so does the owner's, the manager's, the specialist's, and the shampoo technician's.

In the 1950s, understanding these team-power and we-together-can-do-it insights from the field of Salon Psychology was not necessary because the average salon size at that time was one person. In the twenty-first century, the average salon will house at least five times as many people. Having many professionals in a salon creates new training needs, new skill needs for resolving conflicts and reducing stress, pressures, and excessive competition. Higher emphasis must be placed on team work, community feeling, and encouraging one another. It can start with you!

CATCH THE TEAM FEELING!

To catch the team feeling, think about all of the other ways that everybody contributes to the salon's progress — which means your progress.

Whatever professional responsibilities you have, take a few minutes to walk a mile in the shoes of each professional on your team. Start by thinking about all of the ways a receptionist contributes to the total team. Be a receptionist.

Identify five ways that the receptionist contributes to the total salon:

_____

_____

_____

_____

_____

Share with the receptionist your empathic understanding, and watch how good you make him or her feel.

Now take a few minutes and reflect upon all of the ways the stylist contributes to the total team:

_____

_____

_____

_____

_____

Share with the stylist your empathic understanding of his or her world.

Think of five ways the shampoo technician contributes to the total salon team:

_____

_____

_____

_____

_____

Share with the shampoo technician your empathic understanding of his or her contribution.

Think about how the manager contributes to the total salon team. Walk a mile in the manager's shoes this time:

_____

_____

_____

_____

_____

Share with the manager your understanding of his or her contribution.

Finally, leave your world and go to the the world of an owner — someone who took a lot of money, invested it in a dream, hired people he or she believed in, and built a business. Think about how this person contributes to the total team:

_____

_____

_____

_____

Share with the owner your empathic understanding of his or her world.

Congratulations! You've spent some time in understanding your total team. Now ask yourself, "What can I give to help my fellow team members be successful?" That's the way to make myself successful! It's all part of being a contributing team member.

Give credit and thanks continuously, and watch what happens!

Now You Will Feel Like a Contributing Team Member, and It All Started with You.

PART II

NINE PERSONALITY THEORIES APPLIED TO ACHIEVE SUCCESS IN THE SALON

CHAPTER 7

UNDERSTANDING THE SECRETS OF THE UNCONSCIOUS

FREUD

THE THEORY OF SIGMUND FREUD

Many stylists have heard of Sigmund Freud because his name is a regular part of our language. Perhaps you have heard of Freudian slips, or dream interpretation, or psychoanalysis. Freud played the major role in creating the fields of psychiatry and psychology. It is appropriate that we study the ideas of Freud first. You will learn about some of Freud's insights into the work of the unconscious and how it influences behavior.

Soon You Will Be Able To:

- Relate to why people will sometimes do things that may even hurt themselves.

- Understand the role of the unconscious in affecting your client's personality.

- Recognize times when people are using "defenses," so that you can understand what they are really saying.

THE ROLE OF THE UNCONSCIOUS IN UNDERSTANDING MOTIVATION

Wanda is a talented stylist whose technical skills are far superior to anyone else's. She is an absolute magician with hair. Yet she couldn't keep a styling position in any salon for any extended period of time. In one year alone she worked in four different salons. She would be OK until a manager gave her a suggestion on how she could improve. Then she would grab her tools, storm out of the salon, and go to work in another salon. Soon no one in her town would hire her because she had a reputation for being a hothead. A brilliant career filled with potential was thus spoiled because of personality problems.

Why did she hurt herself, her income, and her future? It certainly can't be explained from a rational or conscious perspective.

Sam, an uptight manager, is almost impossible to work with. His nit-picking perfectionism has his staff on constant attack-alert. He explodes at every mistake and has recently developed an ulcer. After a few staff-members resigned, the owner told Sam to settle down and not drive people so hard. Sam just can't stop. He is his own worst enemy!

Why would Sam continue to be tense about even the smallest mistakes when he saw what it was doing to his people? Why couldn't he just take it easy, especially after the owner, who pays Sam's salary, suggested that he ease up? Certainly Sam's behavior can't be explained logically or at a conscious level.

MOTIVATIONS THAT COME FROM THE UNCONSCIOUS

When we see people acting in what appears to be irrational, illogical, or self-destructive ways, we have to understand that not all behavior is motivated by conscious factors. Some of our motivation comes from the subconscious and some stems from unconscious sources.

Wanda's and Sam's behaviors, for example, don't make sense from a conscious perspective, but let's look a little deeper and understand their actions from an unconscious level.

Wanda was raised by very strict parents who were constantly yelling at her and putting her down. Rules, rules, and more rules were all she experienced in her home. Wanda couldn't wait until she became a stylist so she could move out, and today she rarely goes to see her parents. She resents them for their "bossiness" and "rules." In each of her styling positions, Wanda was OK as long as she wasn't "bossed" by someone else (authority figure). When any authority figure, like a manager or owner, did anything that seemed bossy, she would immediately leave the salon that was "hassling her" and go to work for a competitor. She doesn't make the association between her resentment of her bossy parents and any other person who tries to boss her. Because she doesn't understand it, the real reason is not consciously perceived by her. Motivation in her case exists at an unconscious level.

Sam, the perfectionist salon manager, consciously wants to slow down. He doesn't want an angry or nervous staff or an owner who is starting to become intolerant of him. He certainly doesn't want an ulcer! But he can't stop! Sam grew up in a home where his parents taught him things like "Unless you're perfect, you're worthless" and "Don't ever do anything that you can't do perfectly." Sam could never please his parents no matter what he did. As a child, for example, when Sam brought his report card home with five A's and a B, his parents never praised him but spent all of their time downing him for the B. Sam has made his parents' values of over-perfection a part of himself, and he finds he can never live up to those impossible expectations. He tries to impose these standards on everyone around him in the salon. Sam isn't aware of why he acts the way he does because his motivation lies in his unconscious.

SIGMUND FREUD: THE FATHER OF PSYCHOANALYSIS

Discovery of the importance of unconscious factors in motivation was made by Sigmund Freud, the most significant early figure in the study of psychiatry. Freud worked with very seriously disturbed patients suffering from many disorders but primarily from a disease called hysterical neurosis, which is characterized by a paralysis in some part of the body. As Freud worked with these patients, he discovered that after many hours of counseling, which he called psychoanalysis, they could be led to describe early childhood experiences that were traumatic. When they were able to talk about those experiences and hidden memories as well as wishes buried in their unconscious, they tended to get better. Freud concluded that most behaviors exist at an unconscious level and that many times we do things without our conscious awareness.

A person who overeats despite continuous health warnings from a doctor may be influenced by unconscious factors, such as self-punishment, or fear of losing weight and being attractive, thereby having to face the possible stresses of dating — which he didn't have to worry about as much before.

Someone who is promoted and is perfectly capable of handling the job messes it up. Why? Perhaps in this person's unconscious he doesn't see himself as capable and feels, "My inadequacies will soon be discovered, so I might as well expose myself now and get it over with."

Besides our unconscious, we also have motivations, ideas, and experiences in the subconscious and conscious levels of our minds.

In the conscious mind exists all that we are currently aware of at this moment. Whatever you are thinking about or are moved by right now is part of your conscious mind.

In the subconscious mind exist all of those thoughts and experiences which, although you are not thinking about them at this moment, could still be brought to the surface of your conscious mind. For example, can you remember anything that happened on your last birthday? If you can, it was part of your subconscious.

In the unconscious exist those motivations, ideas, and experiences that are hidden or unavailable to you now but still continue to influence your behavior. Freud felt that the job of psychoanalysis was to make the unconscious become conscious to help a person understand why he acts the way he does when the behavior is illogical or irrational.

UNCONSCIOUS MOTIVATIONS OF THE ID, EGO, AND SUPEREGO

Understanding human behavior from an unconscious perspective is very interesting and, at times, useful. Remember this rule: If you observe behavior that doesn't seem logical or rational, it is possible that it reflects an unconscious motivation. To understand your clients, consider the three parts of a person's mind as first conceived by Freud: the *ID*, the *EGO*, and the *SUPEREGO*.

The id is the part of the human mind that is selfish. It wants only satisfaction for self, knows nothing about responsibility, and acts impulsively without regard to consequences. The id is the part of the personality that humans are born with. Watch a young child who runs across the street to pet a dog, without regard to traffic or any other consequences. He just wants what he wants, right now! Or ask a two-year-old if he wants an ice cream cone today or a hundred dollars tomorrow. The child, driven by the id, will choose the ice cream cone now. The id seeks immediate gratification. The id's only words are *"I WANT NOW."*

The ego is the decision-making part of our personality. It decides whether to listen to the impulsive *I WANT NOW* demands of the id or to listen to the responsible but not-so-much-fun demands of the superego. The ego's decisions form what we call our personality.

The superego is that part of a human's personality that we call the conscience. While we all have the same id, our superegos differ. The id words are "I want now"; the superego's words are "You can't have," "You shouldn't," "You mustn't," and all other commands from our conscience that carry with them guilt, shame, and doubt. The superego starts to develop in the second year of life when parents, and later other authority figures, keep the child from exploring too much, getting hurt, or causing problems by his disregard for consequences.

Our ids are the same; our superegos differ based on how well-adjusted, permissive, or severe our conscience is. A severe conscience creates a harsh superego filled with guilt, shame, and doubt. It produces anxieties, phobias, compulsions, and over-perfection. Poor Sam, our perfectionist salon manager, drove himself to unrealistic lengths because of his demanding superego. He was his own worst enemy.

Clients with Rigid Superegos

Some types of people you may face who reflect a severe *SUPEREGO* include:

1. The compulsive client who blows up at any change.
2. The every-hair-perfectly-in-place person.
3. The apologetic, defensive client.
4. The anxious or tense client.
5. The client who needs routine.
6. The client who needs your approval.
7. The client who fears risking any new style or color.
8. The client who will always be on time but demands to be seen when she arrives. Keep in mind that someone with a harsh superego has a strong conscience.

Clients with Weak Superegos

The opposite of the person with a harsh superego is one who has a weak or permissive superego or conscience. This person is characterized by lack of concern, impulsiveness, and irresponsibility. Some clients you may face who have a weak superego include:

1. The client who is always late.
2. The walk-in.
3. The client who constantly wants an exciting change.
4. The client who changes hairstylists frequently.
5. The client who is bored easily.

THE EGO HAS A VARIETY OF WAYS TO COPE WITH STRESS AND BLOWS TO SELF-ESTEEM

Remember, Freud felt that the ego was the chooser, deciding between the "I want" demands of the id and the "You can't have" or "You shouldn't do" restraints of the superego. The ego also serves another function. In his popular text, *Abnormal Psychology and Modern Life*, James Coleman describes how the ego defends the individual. Coleman writes:

> All of us use ego-defense mechanisms. They are essentially for softening failure, reducing cognitive dissonance, alleviating anxiety, protecting oneself against trauma, and maintaining our feelings of adequacy and personal worth. Thus we must consider them normal adjustive reactions unless they are used to such an extreme degree that they interfere with the maintenance of self-integrity instead of being an aid. . . . These mechanisms or ego defenses are necessary to help us face difficulties in life, but they do have certain drawbacks. They involve a high degree of self-deception and reality distortion and usually are not adaptive in the sense of realistically coping with the adjustment problem. Because defense mechanisms operate on a relatively unconscious level, they are not subject to normal conscious checks and evaluations. In fact, the individual usually resents having his attention called to them, for once they become conscious, they do not serve their defensive purposes so well.

As Coleman points out, everyone uses defense mechanisms, and they are a normal and healthy way of adjusting to stress at an unconscious level.

The disadvantage to the individual is that they are a form of lying to oneself, and consequently, when an individual uses these ego defenses over and over, he may lose touch. The student of Salon Psychology needs to be aware of ways to cope with self-esteem blows, pressures, and stresses. The healthiest way, and a way of avoiding ego defenses, is to face reality — face the situation head-on, and deal with the task without any deceptive ego defense.

LET'S COMPARE TASK-ORIENTED REACTIONS WITH EGO-DEFENSE REACTIONS

Task-oriented reactions to stress, rejection, criticism, or blows to self-esteem are those that are aimed at realistically meeting the demands of the situation. Ego-defense reactions are aimed at deceiving oneself to soften the setback of reality. Task reaction faces the situation and deals with it through a plan for attack, withdrawal, or compromise. The ego reaction distorts reality, denies reality, or deceives oneself about self and reality.

Let's consider some ego-defense reactions and observe how each distorts or denies reality and then compare them to task-oriented reactions.

Denial of Reality. Denial is the unconscious escaping, avoiding, or ignoring of unpleasant facts and situations in our environment. We avoid criticism, refuse to face a problem as if it didn't exist, procrastinate, refuse to face unpleasant situations, or get sick instead of taking on a responsibility in which we could fail.

Fantasy. In fantasy, not only do we deny reality, but we reconstruct our own. We fall for get-rich-quick schemes when not facing the fact that we are broke; we accept flattery easily or we imagine ourselves as sports heroes after committing an error that loses the game.

Rationalization. Rationalization is giving a "good" reason instead of the true reason for our behavior to help us justify our actions. A politician who gets caught stealing gets angry and says, "Everybody does it; I just got caught," thus attempting to justify a wrong action. A stylist who is always late explains that there were no clients in the salon anyway. A client who doesn't show up and doesn't cancel her appointment and is faced with a minimal fee for not calling justifies her anger by saying she had to wait the previous time in the salon. The boy who asks a girl to dance and is turned down rationalizes to himself that he didn't want to dance with her anyway — a "good" reason instead of the true reason. A task-oriented reaction from the boy would have been to face the reality, "She said 'No' so I'll simply ask another girl!"

Projection. Projection is another interesting ego-defense reaction to stress and blows to self-esteem. It involves projecting our shortcomings, mistakes, and wrongdoings onto others. A client complains about a haircut and the stylist explains, "Your hair is of a poor quality. There's nothing anybody could do with it." A salon is having a hard go of it, and the manager explains that it's because of the location, or too-high prices. In both cases, note how a task-oriented reaction would differ: In Instance 1, the complaining client, the stylist listens to understand the client, learns more about her type hair, and finds the most effective products, styles, perms, or colors. In Instance 2, the salon manager using a task-oriented reaction finds a way to build business despite poor location and high salon prices, which are projections or excuses.

Displacement. Displacement transfers an emotion felt toward someone — occasionally self — onto another person or object that is safer. A stylist who has a bad day at the salon (complaining clients, a manager who yells at her) holds it all in and lets it build until she gets home. Then she explodes at her poor husband, who was excited about seeing her. She displaced her hostility onto him because he was "safe." A task-oriented reaction would have been to face herself and simply say, "Today is over; what did I learn from it that I can use to make tomorrow better?"

We have seen that healthier task-oriented reactions to stress and setbacks include facing reality directly and responsibly: coping by deciding whether to "attack" in order to change the situation; withdraw, accept it and move on; or compromise with reality. In a sense, this is very similar to the "Serenity Prayer" on adjustment, which says, "God grant me the courage to change the things I can, the serenity to accept the things I can't, and the wisdom to know the difference." The opposite type of reaction to stress or blows to self-esteem is called ego-defensive. Reactions in this category are those that deny or distort reality and deceive a person about himself. They include denial, fantasy, rationalization, projection, and displacement of emotions.

When facing any situation in which you feel rejected, criticized, blamed, or any other negative emotion, remember this chapter on how the ego adapts and see if you can use a healthy coping mechanism by facing reality head-on using a task-oriented reaction. Each time you do so, you take a giant step toward getting to know your real self, taking responsible charge of your life, reducing emotional stress the healthy way, and gaining the respect of those around you!

SUMMARY

You have just been introduced to Sigmund Freud's personality theory of the unconscious. Freud discovered that many things we do are caused by motivations that we are not aware of; they are at the unconscious level. Whenever we observe illogical or irrational behavior, chances are that the motive for it exists at an unconscious, unaware level. We have two other levels of motivation: the conscious and the subconscious. Freud felt that the task of psychoanalysis was to make the unconscious become conscious so that a person could take charge of his life and destiny!

Freud felt that personality was formed by an interplay of three imaginary aspects of our mind. The id is the impulsive, selfish part of us; the superego is the conscience that keeps us on track; and the ego is the decider which chooses to listen either to the id or to the superego. From the decisions the ego makes, we develop our unique personalities.

The ego has another function. It also serves the role of protecting our self-esteem, assisting us in coping with stress and alleviating our anxieties. It does this in two ways when we face a threatening situation. First, the ego can respond with a positive task-oriented reaction by facing reality head-on and finding the best solution: Attack, withdraw, or compromise! A second way the ego responds is a little less healthy although certainly more common. The ego-defense reaction to stress or blows to self-esteem involves denying or distorting reality: lying to oneself to justify behavior, creating a fantasy world to escape an unpleasantry, rationalizing, placing on others the blame for our own shortcomings, or taking out on a "safer" person the negative emotions we feel toward another.

By understanding the role of unconscious motivations in our behavior, we can take charge of our lives. We can stop deceiving and defeating ourselves. (Freud made a great contribution to the understanding of what makes people tick by making us aware of our unconscious and how to control it.)

Let's now turn to another personality theorist who will add to your ideas about how personality is shaped and how it can be changed. You will see a real breath of fresh air in Carl Jung's spiritual theory of personality shaping.

CHAPTER 8

BUILDING
DEEP
CONNECTIONS
WITH PEOPLE
THROUGH
YOUR
COLLECTIVE
UNCONSCIOUS

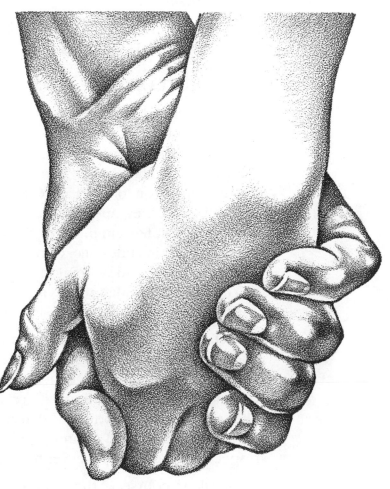

THE THEORY OF CARL JUNG

Why is it that you can meet someone who lives in another city or even in another culture and find yourself more "in tune" with him or her than with someone from your own neighborhood whom you have known for twenty years? Carl Jung has some answers to that and other questions which involve the mysterious and the spiritual.

Soon You Will Be Able To:

- Understand why there is something about some people you connect with immediately.

- Unleash the powers of your collective unconscious to reach your dreams.

- Feel part of the worldwide spirit of hairstylists who are linked with you and want you to be linked with them.

THE SPIRIT OF THE SALON

Each weekend that I have the opportunity to conduct seminars and lectures with hairstylists on Salon Psychology, I am deeply touched by something I experience. Whether I am with stylists in Manchester, Wichita, Chicago, Milwaukee, Dallas, Edmonton, or Salt Lake City — even Auckland, New Zealand, or Sydney, Australia — I am touched with the common spirit I feel in them. At the very deepest level, a cosmetologist in Hinesville, Georgia, who has taken the time to seek advanced study in Salon Psychology, is linked to the spirit of a stylist in Madison, Wisconsin, who also wants to advance herself and her profession. And they have never met!

Each class of cosmetologists reveals to me the same shared concerns, questions, love of the profession, caring, and desire to become even better. I see these similarities whether north or south of the equator. To me it's refreshing and inspiring — like seeing a whole worldwide community drawing from the same energy source of meaning and purpose and mutual respect. Yet these people never meet except in spirit!

I speak, of course, of those "early risers" of the profession who are the real pros. Sadly, many hairstylists who are down on themselves and their job never really experience such spirit. It is fortunate for me that the professionals I work with are the forerunners, those who are the energy behind the evolution of the salon profession. Each week I reassure them that they, the leaders of the new direction, are closer in spirit to like-minded people on the other side of the world than they are to those who don't share the same spirit even if they work together in the same salon! Some people live in the same city; some live in the same spirit. Who are closer?

We at Matrix University have a dream of someday bringing all of our students of Salon Psychology together so that they can experience the same sense of "connectedness" that I have the opportunity to feel. Perhaps by the time you read this book it will already have happened. Can you imagine the experience of community that day?

Until then, you can exhilarate yourself with a feeling of being connected, together, part of a worldwide movement of spirits plugged into a boundless energy source. You can never be alone, and your spirits can always be lifted by this universal energy — which takes us to the famous personality theorist, Carl Jung, and his beautiful concept of the collective unconscious.

THE COLLECTIVE UNCONSCIOUS: YOUR ENERGY SOURCE FOR ANYTHING YOU NEED!

How can the common spirit, the common link between professional hairstylists throughout the world, be explained if they have never even met? Jung, having learned much from Freud, took Freud's concept of the unconscious and expanded on it, giving it more life and strength. Interested in anthropology and the study of culture, Jung was fascinated with how all cultures, no matter where they are, have many common elements. Every culture has some form of god, totem or worship, government, heroes, and villains. This is true whether they have lived in jungles or skyscrapers. Jung believed that this demonstrated a power of influence stronger than the learning habits of a specific culture. That universal power of influence Jung called the collective unconscious.

It's collective because whether from Afghanistan, Des Moines, or Moscow, we share the same humanity; it's unconscious because we are ordinarily not aware of its presence. The collective unconscious is the the place where everything that has taken place in the world before us gathers. It has little to do with a given place because everyone has the same collective spiritual unity. That's why you are sometimes immediately in tune with another you've never met.

Jung felt that the collective unconscious held possibilities which were locked away from the conscious mind, as well as the wisdom and experience of uncounted centuries.

In your collective unconscious exist the same wisdom that was available to the wisest human being that ever lived, the strength of the strongest, and the courage of the most courageous. It is genetically programmed, according to Jung. It needs to be cultivated and refined by you. Any problem that you face in life has its answer inside you in the form of every experience every human has ever had. You can unleash the power of your collective unconscious by dipping into this universal pool of unlimited potential — draw new ideas, plug into sources waiting for your attention. It's all there inside you at this moment.

USING YOUR COLLECTIVE UNCONSCIOUS

1. Trust the vibes you get that you can't quite explain about how to design a client's hair. You may be totally surprised by the client's response that he or she had some similar thoughts.

2. Realize that no matter how much you feel another person (a first-time client) appears to be a stranger to you, you are linked. There were times with a doctor, teacher, or lawyer when you were a first-time client.

3. No matter what you face in life, walk away to dip into your collective unconscious to draw from its richness through ages of civilization, and use the resources of the others who are just like you.

4. And then, give back to the future of the collective unconscious.

YOUR CONTRIBUTION TO THE COLLECTIVE UNCONSCIOUS

The genius Buckminster Fuller asserted, "There are no passengers on this spaceship earth — we are all crew!" Just as every living being throughout the ages contributes to this pool of collective unconscious, every experience of yours adds to it, furthering life, even way beyond the moment.

I once heard a story of a youngster who was walking along

the beach in the early morning and picked up starfish that had washed up at night. He flung them back into the sea. As he continued his mission, he was stopped by a cynic who asked what he was doing. The youngster replied, "I'm saving these starfish from being baked in the sun and dying, by taking them home to the sea."

"But there are thousands of miles of beaches in the world and millions of starfish that get washed up each day. How in the world do you think your work can make any difference at all?" The youth continued, picked up the next starfish, and as he flung it into the heavy foam of the sea answered, "It'll make a difference to this one!"

Each day of your life, your work does makes a difference, in a very practical way, in the life of those you serve. In a metaphysical way, according to Carl Jung, you are also contributing to the betterment of every generation that will follow. Your experience adds to the pool of the collective unconscious, the spirit of the world!

SUMMARY OF THE COLLECTIVE UNCONSCIOUS AND THE SPIRIT OF THE SALON PROFESSION

Carl Jung was a breath of fresh air after Freud's ideas about the unconscious' being a dark, frightening part of our personality. Jung saw the collective unconscious as a powerful pool comprised of every experience any human ever had, genetically programmed within him, to be used by cultivating it. No matter what we face, Jung said that the answers are within us. Creativity is housed in the collective unconscious.

Hairstylists of the world are linked, not only in their collective unconscious but also in a very special spirit of our time, and a professional desire to grow, belong, and care. They are linked even when they haven't met. That's why the linkage is spiritual.

Each professional day in the salon, every hairstylist by every action contributes to the pool of the world's collective unconscious and contributes to the evolution of the salon profession.

Now, let's turn to another psychiatrist, Alfred Adler, who is gaining in popularity today because of his "practical" theories.

CHAPTER 9

PEOPLE ARE
THE REASONS
WE DO
WHAT
WE DO

THE THEORY OF ALFRED ADLER

Alfred Adler was an optimist who believed in the social
nature of people. At our deepest level, Adler felt, we have a
need for attention and recognition as well as needs for
belonging and contributing to something greater than ourselves. What we do is best understood by observing our
interaction with the people around us. It was Adler who
created a very popular word now used in the salon, "lifestyle." To Adler our lifestyle was our way of trying to fit in
with others.

Soon You Will Be Able To:

- Understand the five major reasons why people act the way they do.

- Better see through people who are rebellious or sympathy-seeking or who have a constant need for attention or even people who constantly brag.

- Deal with the unruly child or the continually late client.

YOU CAN BE THE DIFFERENCE IN ANOTHER PERSON'S LIFE

Sigmund Freud believed that humans are motivated by unconscious factors. Carl Jung thought that "spiritual" factors are the determiners of our personality. Alfred Adler argued that human beings are, above all else, motivated by social factors. To really understand a person's lifestyle, we need to see that person with other people. That is why the same person working unproductively in one salon can be put into another salon's social setting and function with flying colors! That's why the same client may act in different ways with different stylists. In this chapter you will be given a third way, perhaps the most practical one so far, of understanding why people act the way they do.

FIVE WAYS OF UNDERSTANDING HUMAN BEHAVIOR

Adler showed us how we can understand and be successful with others just by remembering five things. Memorize this roadmap, and it will lead you to a better understanding of human behavior.

1. **People act out of the way they — not I — look at life.** This is called their "private logic." All of their behavior makes sense if we take some time to listen to how they see the situation. If in a person's private logic he believes that he was just bitten by a snake, from a psychological perspective he will act no differently from a person who actually was bitten by a snake.

Disagreements in life occur because of differing private logics. Failure to resolve differences is simply a failure to take some time to understand how the other person is viewing the situation. Even your worst enemy believes, in his own private logic, that he is correct. Benedict Arnold was both an American traitor and a British hero, depending on whose private logic one uses! Any call at home plate — safe or out — is seen differently through the home or visiting team's private logic.

When we understand another person through High-Touch Empathy (Chapter 1), we enter his world, his private logic, and begin real communication.

2. **People are socially rooted, and all of their behavior is geared to fulfilling these social needs: attention, recognition, feeling significant, contributing, and belonging.** Happy, successful living occurs because our social needs are fulfilled. However, when our social needs are not met, we become discouraged. Such *discouragement* is seen in these faulty behaviors:

   a. **Rebellion.** "I'll get attention and power the wrong way since I can't get it by doing the right things."

   b. **Sympathy seeking.** "Pity me and take care of me because I am so unimportant."

   c. **Constant need to be the center stage.** "Unless everybody is noticing me, I'm unimportant."

   d. **Withdrawal from others.** "I'll act as if I don't need you before you act as if you don't need me."

   e. **Jealousy of others who are getting attention.** "She's not so hot." **Even dishonesty:** "I have dozens of trophies at home for winning hair shows in other cities."

   f. **Bragging in a faulty attempt to gain respect.** "Sure, I could have been the manager too if I had acted the way she did."

Keep in mind that, according to Adler, people have a strong need for attention and feeling important. When their private logic concludes that they are not respected, they become discouraged and exhibit one or more of these symptoms. Discouraged behaviors are signs saying, "I don't feel as if I fit in," or "I don't feel important," or "I don't feel accepted and noticed when I do the right thing. I can get more attention by doing the wrong thing. I would rather even be punished than not noticed. And I know that you will notice me if I am disruptive."

3. **All behavior is directed toward achieving some goal.** When we observe a person's behavior, we can ask what goal the person is trying to achieve by his actions. Get-my-own-way emotions are used as a means of reaching that goal.

Adler saw emotions as something that worked for us as children in helping us get what we wanted from others. Many times, even as adults, we continue to use those emotions to get our way. For example, Adlerians call tears "water power." If water power worked for a child (to get a new toy or avoid the responsibilities of homework), this faulty behavior was reinforced. The child then continues to "use" tears to try to manipulate red traffic lights, teachers, friends, and yes, even bosses. Often the adult becomes frustrated because in his private logic he concludes that it should work. It worked before!

By the same token, if temper tantrums worked for a child to get his way with Mom and Dad, he will continue to use that faulty behavior whenever he wants something. Unfortunately, red lights have little regard for one's private logic.

According to Adler, people are socially rooted, operate out of their own private logic, and use their emotions to achieve their goals.

4. **While people are socially rooted, they also have a need to be special and unique.** I wrote, in *The Motivating Leader*:

In the age of technology, society tried to organize

individuals into a "this" category or a "that" category. This was done so that people would fit into the finite mind of the computer, limited in its ability to give every person the uniqueness that was rightfully his or hers. But whenever we attempt to quantify people, we disqualify their uniqueness.

The ultimate expression of High Touch is to know something special and unique about each person. In our High-Tech age, if you do this, you'll be a breath of fresh air and will help to fulfill your clients' and friends' social need to feel unique.

5. **People function holistically; that is, they are not viewed as mind and body or hair and heart but as total people. The total self is encompassed in the term "lifestyle."** In their book, *The Individual Psychology of Alfred Adler,* authors Heinz and Rowena Ansbacher describe lifestyle as comprising, in addition to goals, the individual's opinion of himself and the world, as well as his unique way of striving for goal achievement in his particular situation. Thus, people operate out of private logic in a way that they believe will gain them attention from others (goal), and they strive for uniqueness. How someone attempts to achieve these social goals is called his lifestyle.

UNDERSTANDING PEOPLE THROUGH ADLERIAN PSYCHOLOGY

Situation 1: Becky was a great stylist in a two-person salon and was offered a job in the town's top salon. Connie worked in the same salon and was considered the best stylist around. She also worked as a platform artist sometimes on weekends. Becky was excited, but when she started in her new chair, she heard the owner, manager, and many clients praising Connie's work and comparing Becky to Connie. Becky got discouraged and started to rebel by denigrating Connie and breaking into tears. She soon was asked to leave the salon. She lost her fine job — a great stylist in one salon, a rebel in another.

If you take just a few minutes and reread Adler's five ways of understanding people, you'll see how much you actually know of what makes people tick. Jot in some things that you think took place in Becky's "private logic" — why she acted the way she did, and maybe even how the situation could have been avoided if others had understood Becky's needs. Have fun with it.

_____

_____

_____

_____

_____

Situation 2: Debby, a three-year-old, acted responsibly in the salon most of the time. No one really noticed her until one week she started to run around and pick up shears. All of a sudden people were giving her attention. Each time she comes into the salon with her mother, she seems to get worse. Some say it's a stage she's going through. Knowing Adler's ideas, how might you handle Debby's attention-seeking behavior?

_____

_____

_____

_____

_____

While there are many possible explanations for both situations, perhaps you saw Becky, in Situation 1, as discouraged and feeling unimportant after having been the star at another salon. Her discouragement came out in the form of rebellion and tears. Someone just looking at her on the surface may have thought her a "pain," but if you look closely, you can see discouragement. The problem might have been avoided if everyone had been sensitive enough not to compare her work with Connie's; they could have found out what was "unique" about Becky and helped her, as the newcomer, feel that she belonged. Someone might have helped her show what she could contribute to the social setting of the salon.

In Situation 2, little Debby wasn't getting her needs for attention fulfilled by "being good." When people don't notice us for doing the right thing, there is one sure way of getting noticed — doing the wrong thing. Debby found out that misbehavior gave her more attention than responsible behavior. By giving recognition and attention for responsible behavior, the problem could have been avoided in Debby's case, too.

Perhaps you, in the salon or in class, would like to consider some of the tough clients you have to deal with. Use Adler's five points.

_____

_____

_____

_____

_____

SUMMARY OF SOCIAL REASONS TO EXPLAIN HUMAN BEHAVIOR

Freud, Jung, and Adler laid the foundation for the field of psychology in the early 1900s. They disagreed in many ways: Freud emphasized the role of the unconscious; Jung stressed the importance of spiritual factors on behavior; Adler believed that behavior can be best understood as being goal-driven (what a person wants to achieve in a particular social setting). A person's private logic or his unique way of looking at a situation is the starting point from which to understand his behavior. Once we understand his private logic, we better understand the person.

We also gain the advantage of understanding how a person would probably act in any given situation. We can thus see more effective ways of communicating with him and building a successful relationship.

Disruptive or irresponsible behaviors are faulty attempts to achieve goals. We can encourage more responsible behaviors by noticing people when they act appropriately and ignoring (not giving attention to) negative behaviors. Adler's ideas, as you can see, are practical and usable in the salon.

CHAPTER 10

ACTUALIZING YOUR OWN AND YOUR CLIENT'S POTENTIAL

THE THEORY OF ABRAHAM MASLOW

ACTUALIZATION is the process of moving toward becoming all that one is capable of being. The little seed, when actualized, becomes the giant oak. *Actual*-ization is the *real*-ization of one's potential.

Soon You Will Be Able To:

- Develop the qualities of the world's healthiest, happiest people by actualizing your potential.

- Help your clients to look the best they can (actualize their potential).

- See how what you do as a stylist on outer image is exactly what a psychologist does on inner image.

USE THE BEST AS MODELS OF YOUR POSSIBILITIES

A SELF-ACTUALIZED PERSON is one who is in the process of reaching toward actualization, the ultimate expression of human life, using all of his or her potential.

Albert Einstein changed the convictions of physicists who once believed that Sir Isaac Newton's ideas were unshakably accurate. Many leading cosmetologists have played important roles in transforming old concepts of their profession.

Abraham H. Maslow, our psychologist in this chapter, transformed the thoughts of the psychological community. Maslow outrightly challenged the ideas of Sigmund Freud, which suggested that people can't change after six or seven years of age. Maslow showed how change is possible for anyone. He shifted the thinking of psychologists who once looked at patients to see "What's wrong here?" or "What disease does this person suffer from?" to looking for the "hidden potential and assets in people." Instead of studying how low human beings can slip, Maslow was interested in studying the ceilings of human possibility.

In his book, *The Farther Reaches of Human Nature,* Maslow wrote:

> If you want to answer the question how tall can the human species grow, then obviously it is well to pick out the ones who are already tallest and study them. If we want to know how fast a human being can run, then it is no use to average out the speed of a sample of the population; it is far better to collect Olympic gold-medal winners and see how well they can do. If we want to

know the possibilities for spiritual growth, value growth, or moral development in human beings, then I maintain that we can learn the most by studying our most moral, ethical, or saintly people.

On the whole I think that it is fair to say that human history is a record of the ways in which human nature has been sold short. The highest possibilities of human nature have practically always been underrated. Even when good specimens — the saints, the sages, and the great leaders of history — have been available for study, the temptation too often has been to consider them not human, but supernaturally endowed.

USE THE BEST AS MODELS OF YOUR POSSIBILITIES.

DARE TO TEST THOSE LIMITS YOU PUT ON YOURSELF

Freud taught us we were afraid of our worst; Maslow taught us we too often are afraid of our best! Maslow labeled this defense the "fear of one's own greatness" or the "evasion of one's destiny" or the "running away from one's own best talents." He believed, "We fear our highest possibilities (as well as our lowest ones). We are generally afraid to become that which we can glimpse in our most perfect moments, under the most perfect conditions, under conditions of greatest courage. We enjoy and even thrill to the godlike possibilities we see in ourselves in such peak moments, and yet we simultaneously shiver with weakness, awe, and fear before these very same possibilities."

Maslow frequently asked his students, "Which of you in this class hopes to write the great American novel or be a senator, a governor, or the president?" His students would look around to see if anyone else had raised his hand. The professor then turned to his students and asked why they were looking elsewhere for greatness. And looking each of his students squarely in the eye he asked, "If not you, then who else?"

The self-actualized person answers that question by saying, "It's up to me to develop my potential to the fullest. Let me test my limits; let me experience where the ceilings really are in my life by living my life fully — not by backing away from my total potential."

THE ROAD TO SELF-ACTUALIZATION: MASLOW'S HIERARCHY OF NEEDS

Maslow concluded that every person's behavior could best be understood as being motivated from one of five different levels of needs. From lowest to highest level, there are *PHYSIOLOGICAL, SAFETY OR SECURITY, SOCIAL OR BELONGING, SELF-ESTEEM,* and *SELF-ACTUALIZATION* needs.

At the bottom level of Maslow's Hierarchy of Needs is the *physiological level.* Here the individual is motivated by only one thing: satisfaction of a physiological need, the most important one being hunger. Someone at this lowest level of motivation isn't interested in friends, isn't interested in job excellence or self-actualization. At the physiological level he is interested only in food. All of his behaviors can be understood as motivated by seeking to satisfy that need.

When physiological needs are satisfied, he is motivated at the next step on Maslow's Hierarchy: *safety or security needs.* At Level 2, a person is seeking either material safety (a shelter, apartment, or home in which to live) or psychological security (feeling protected from threats). The first two levels of need are called "survival levels," and all humans have them in common with all members of the animal world.

When physiological and safety/security needs are satiated, one moves up the hierarchy to Level 3, the *social or belonging level.* With a full stomach and a feeling of security, a person is now motivated to build friendships, contribute to others, and belong socially. This could also be considered a phase in which one conforms to others' standards.

At Level 4, motivation moves to *self-esteem needs.* Here an individual starts to become a unique person who has developed a sense of "self" apart from just being like everyone else. At the self-esteem level, he takes pride in his work and pride in what he can do. He is on the threshold of the ultimate expression of a human being, psychologically speaking.

At the top of Maslow's Hierarchy is *self-actualization*, Level 5. At this level, a person is moving toward expressing himself fully in life and becoming what he is capable of being — actualizing his potential. Let's look further at the Maslow Hierarchy of Needs.

MASLOW'S HIERARCHY OF NEEDS TO EXPLAIN WHAT MOTIVATES A PERSON

5. SELF-ACTUALIZATION

4. SELF-ESTEEM

3. SOCIAL/BELONGING

2. SAFETY/SECURITY

1. PHYSIOLOGICAL

We tend to jump around the scale during the course of the routine day—for example, when we get hungry. But in general we are more or less consistently at one level. The starving people of the world continually function at Level 1. By looking at the different levels that motivate people, we see a few interesting things. Conflicts often arise in salons because the owner may be functioning at the self-actualization or self-esteem level (taking pride in work or business) while the new stylist is functioning at the safety/security level (trying to get enough money together for an apartment). What motivates each is different. If the salon is in danger of bankruptcy, the owner might be at the safety/security level while the young stylist, upset that she may lose her friends if the shop closes, is at the social/belonging level.

This also explains why stylists can succeed with some clients and not with others. A stylist at the self-actualizing level is creative, not afraid of change; and a client at the social/belonging level (conformity) wants to look like all of her friends.

We will shortly return to this hierarchy and talk about how stylists can actualize their own as well as their clients' potential. In order to do that, we have to understand the qualities present in the ultimate human being, the Self-Actualized Person. Understanding these fourteen qualities which Maslow found were present in the happiest, most fulfilled person will be our guide on the Road to Actualization! These qualities Maslow recorded in his book, *Motivation and Personality.*

FOURTEEN CHARACTERISTICS OF SELF-ACTUALIZED PEOPLE

1. **More efficient perception of reality and more comfortable relationship with reality.** Self-actualized people are secure and do not have to twist facts to fit their own emotional needs, nor do they have to lie to themselves or inflate their own value. They face life as it is.

2. **Acceptance of self, others, and nature.** They don't need to be reassured that their way is right, so self-actualized people don't try to force others to think as they do. They accept the world — don't get upset with rain; simply get an umbrella! As you can see, while most of the world is wasting time with unacceptance, self-actualized people use their energies in less defensive, more constructive ways.

3. **Spontaneity.** Self-actualized people are secure enough to not be afraid of being wrong. They spontaneously share on a moment-to-moment basis the things that are on their minds and in their hearts. Sometimes their spontaneity isn't understood by others; sometimes it's not liked by others. But the self-actualized person is full of surprises.

4. **Problem centering.** Ego-centered people are totally wrapped up in how others see them. Self-actualized people are not ego centered but goal centered. They are more interested in solving a problem than in looking good. Consequently, when something doesn't work out, instead of getting frustrated or defensive, they simply go back to the problem and try a different way. The self-actualized stylist doesn't give up after a client complains but just tries to solve the problem.

5. **The need for privacy at times.** The self-actualized person is not afraid to be by himself at times in order to think about his life, set goals, and make plans. He doesn't need people in order to feel OK.

6. **Autonomy — independence of culture and environment.** The self-actualized person trusts himself and his judgments. He doesn't, for example, eat three meals a day because everybody else does or because one is supposed to. He decides what's right for himself and trusts it.

7. **Continued freshness of appreciation.** Self-actualizing people have the wonderful capacity to appreciate again and again, freshly and naively, the basic good things of life — with awe, wonder, and even ecstasy — however stale these experiences might have become to others.

8. **Expanded viewpoint.** Much more frequently than the general population, self-actualized people describe experiences in which they feel limitless horizons opening up to their vision, feel at one with the universe, powerful, and overwhelmed with great ecstasy. These special moments Maslow came to call "Peak Experiences."

9. **Social interest.** They have a deep feeling for all human beings, not just those who are "like me."

10. **Deeper and more meaningful interpersonal relationships.** Because of their dislike for superficiality, they are genuine. You can get to know self-actualized people easily. But they only seek out others who also are nondefensive and genuine. This accounts for the fact that they don't have a lot of surface friends, but a few very meaningful ones.

11. **Democratic character structure.** They don't judge people by education, class, color, religion, sex, or what kinds of cars they drive. The self-actualized person meets people candidly and doesn't need superficial roles to interfere. The self-actualized salon owner sees

the manager, stylists, and the rest of the staff as equal in a human way.

12. **Discrimination between means and ends.** Unlike students who ask, "Will this be on the test?" and think, "Then I will study it," self-actualized people do not see learning as a means to an end (I'll learn so I get good grades) but rather see each day of learning as a reward in itself.

13. **Creativeness.** Because they are not afraid of making mistakes, they bring out the best in themselves creatively. At times they march to a different drummer because of their creativity, but it is self-actualized people who make all of the breakthroughs for the world. The creative hairstylist isn't afraid to wear new hairstyles or create new hairstyles on her clients.

14. **Resistance to enculturation.** Self-actualized people don't do things just because others do. Again, they trust their inner judgment.

Review this list and jot down a few of your own thoughts about self-actualized people:

_____

_____

_____

_____

_____

ACTUALIZING YOUR CLIENT'S APPEARANCE POTENTIAL

You now have a good feeling for the qualities of the self-actualized person. In general, he or she is genuine, not phony; accepting, not manipulative; and creative, not defensive. With this knowledge, you are in an excellent position to see how to actualize your own and your client's potential.

To do so, look again at this list of Maslow's Hierarchy of Needs:

5. Self-Actualization Needs: The qualities just addressed, plus when having confidence in someone, will trust that person as an expert.

4. Self-Esteem Needs: Wants to express unique self.

3. Social/Belonging Needs: Conformity, acceptance, needs to be like others.

2. Safety/Security Needs: Shelter, freedom from threat, just gets by.

1. Physiological Needs: Hunger, thirst; if satisfied, goes to Level 2.

What a psychologist does is try to help his clients move up the ladder toward self-actualization or the fulfillment of the inner self. If a person who comes to a psychologist is feeling OK at Level 2, the psychologist encourages his growth to Level 3 and so on up. That's how a psychologist helps people grow!

What you do as a cosmetologist involves the same process and the same hierarchy model; the only difference is that you help people move toward actualization of their outer potential! Here is how you can recognize what level each client is on from an outer-image perspective:

Person at Level 1 (physiological) wouldn't even be coming to a salon.

Person at Level 2 (safety/security) is coming to the salon just to get by. Mom or Dad has said, "Your hair is too long; get it cut!" or the client decides to risk "Just a trim!" This client obviously does not get all of the benefits from the salon that she could and obviously is far from actualization or realization of her outer potential. Perhaps at your professional suggestion or in the safety of the High-Touch relationship you have built up, one day she will come in requesting something more. This is an important moment, one in which you are helping someone to move up the hierarchy and closer to actualization.

Person at Level 3 (social/belonging) is ready for something new but only if it is safe. How can you be fairly sure what you do will be safe and "approved of by others?" Well, simply make her haircut similar to those you do for her friends. Can you see that this is a higher level benefit than Level 2? But can you see also that this person still has some way to go to achieve actualization or trust in self?

Person at Level 4 (self-esteem) no longer needs approval of others and now wants to express self. "This is what I like," she says, trusting self. You have come a long way if you started her off at Level 2. Aren't the qualities she is now showing much more like the fourteen qualities of the self-actualized person than the person at Level 2?

Person at Level 5 (self-actualization) expresses the ultimate professional relationship between client and stylist. So much trust has been built up through good empathic communication and understanding of lifestyle that this self-actualized client turns to you, the stylist, and says, "You know me — what do you think?"

There are no limits to how you can help this client, who has no limits. *You actualize the client's outer-image potential.* In the process you are actualizing yourself!

SUMMARY OF ACTUALIZING YOUR OWN AND YOUR CLIENT'S POTENTIAL

Psychologist Abraham H. Maslow was like a breath of fresh air because of his interest in studying healthy, happy, fulfilled people to find out why they got so much out of life. He called these people *SELF-ACTUALIZERS* because they were actualizing their potential just as the acorn's actualized potential was expressed in the sturdy giant oak.

In this chapter we discussed Maslow's Hierarchy of Needs, needs that motivate people. The ultimate need, when all others were fulfilled, was *SELF-ACTUALIZATION*. The fourteen major qualities of the self-actualized person were discussed and how what a psychologist does with clients in helping them move toward actualization of their inner potential is the same process that you as a stylist engage in to help your clients move toward actualization of their outer potential. When you actualize a client's potential by helping the client go up the hierarchy from "Just a trim" to "Knowing me, what do you think?" you reach the ultimate professional destination — self-actualization yourself!

CHAPTER 11

CLIENT ANXIETY AND RESISTANCE TO IMAGE CHANGE

THE THEORY OF ROLLO MAY

Freud addressed the unconscious; Jung, the collective unconscious that links us all; Adler saw us as socially rooted; and Maslow told us we all have a need for self-actualization of our potential. Rollo May spent his life studying the anxieties of changing and growing. These ideas have important implications for you, the stylist, because when someone changes hairstyles, she is taking a chance — and change brings anxiety. How do you best help her over the anxicty of change?

Soon You Will Be Able To:

- Know why some clients keep on getting the same old boring trim when you could be giving them so much more.

- Help clients turn their negative anxieties about a new look into anticipation of a new look.

- Recognize your clients' low and high readiness points for change.

CLIENT ANXIETY: THE STYLIST'S CHIEF ENEMY THAT BLOCKS CLIENT MAXIMUM APPEARANCE

Any person in the world who is given an unlimited opportunity to look as good as she could would unquestionably take that opportunity. Right? Unbelievable — but, no, not right!

Gloria is a New England dentist. She was a bookworm in school, had no social life, and never dated in high school. She was homely; she never wore any makeup, and her hair was untidy. Her parents had little money to buy her attractive clothing. Gloria had a positive self-image about her intellectual, academic self, but a very negative self-image about her physical appearance. After winning a scholarship and completing dental school, Gloria opened her own dental practice. All of a sudden, this person accustomed to living with little income was earning money way beyond her dreams. She could afford to have many things she never had before, yet she didn't go to a salon to have her hair and makeup done. Why?

Unconsciously, Gloria had a self-image of being unattractive, not a very positive feeling. Nevertheless, she felt comfortable with her negative image because at least she knew who she was. If she were to go to a salon and let the stylist improve her appearance, Gloria would have to cope with the anxiety of confusion: "A homely person is a phony if she tries to look beautiful — it really wouldn't be me, and what new problems might I then have to face? Maybe I'd be asked out on a date, and I wouldn't know how to act!"

Wouldn't it be easier for Gloria to just avoid the anxiety of image change and go about her life, comfortable being the only person she knows herself to be? Certainly.

As you can see, everyone who is given the unlimited opportunity to look her absolute best does not necessarily take that opportunity — if the new look and the new image provoke anxiety. The person then builds up resistance to changing her appearance.

What is the anxiety of change? What can a stylist do to assist the client in overcoming it?

ANXIETY: A NECESSARY PART OF CHANGE

Every day throughout the world hairstylists are changing people by changing their appearance. Just looking at before and after photos of stylists' work makes it very clear that the skills and tools of a hairstylist produce anything from a small to a dramatic change in how people look. Any time in life we stand on the verge of change, peering into uncertainty, we are immersed in mixed feelings of excitement/fear, love/hate, desire to move forward/urge to retreat, giddiness/dread. These feelings are called anxiety. Anxiety accompanies change as a shadow accompanies you on a bright sunny day. There is no avoiding it, no getting around it. We all face anxiety every time we make changes in our lives. However, what varies from person to person is the view each one takes toward the anxiety involved in change. If it could be seen that anxiety is actually a positive force indicating growth, newness, and change, people would be more willing to flow with change and to grow into a "new image"!

Far too many people retreat when facing change because they don't want the accompanying anxiety. So when that 10:00 of yours, who you know would look super with some bouncy curl in her hair, just asks for a trim, you will understand why. She would rather avoid the uncertainty of change and continue in her known, anxiety-free state. Thus, she isn't looking the best she could because she is misusing anxiety. She sees her feelings of anxiety as a possibility that something might go wrong instead of seeing them as a clue from her body that change is in progress — change that could open up a whole new life for her!

ANXIETY: A FEELING THAT WHISPERS TO US ABOUT NEW POSSIBILITIES

Rollo May, the noted psychoanalyst, saw anxiety as "possibility." No anxiety, no new possibilities! In his popular book, *Freedom and Destiny,* May wrote, "Since personal freedom is a venture down paths we have never traversed before, we can never know ahead of time how the venture will turn out. We leap into the future. Where will we land? With freedom one experiences a dizziness, a feeling of giddiness, a sense of vertigo and dread."

The philosopher Soren Kierkegaard identified anxiety as the cutting edge of change. Otto Rank, another popular psychiatrist, referred to anxiety as the apprehension involved at separation points in our lifetime. Does not a major change in your client's hairstyle reflect a personal change that separates how she expressed herself before from how she will express herself hereafter? The ending of the old way is simply the beginning of a new one!

I once wrote my thoughts about changes and how one can look back, retreat, and withdraw from life when experiencing change or look forward to change and flow with the stream of life. This poem gives a perspective on gaining the future for only the ticket price of letting go of the past.

Endings Are Seeds for Beginnings

All endings are seeds for beginnings;
Tomorrow will come — in due time.
Often in hopelessness lie seeds of hope,
And even a small seed can climb.

But seeds must relinquish their past
On their trip to becoming a tree.
Say, didn't you ever transcend in your life
Prior visions of who you could be?

Each cloud opens up to the sun,
And the low sea will soon reach high tide.
Exits and entrances use the same gate;
Moving through is your ticket to pride.

Two triangles give up themselves
And combine to form one perfect square,
So for every discovery you make in this life,
You must give up some things that were there.

Little choices, big character build;
Tomorrow's pearls are today's grains of sand.
Hear the whispers of seeds growing toward bigger goals
Through the endings of things not so grand.

Caterpillars will some day fly high;
Princes give up their youth to be kings.
The trapeze performer must let go below
To reach after still higher rings.

Yes, you must climb from ruts that engulf you
In order to soar far in flight.
But are not the endings of things that are wrong
The beginnings of things that are right?

You stand at the crossroad, your choice,
Handcuffed by the past or set free.
One path will lead back to the place you have been;
The other, to where you could be.

So rise like the sun in the morn,
Like the wind lifting up silent sea.
And put hope in your heart like a seedling in spring;
Go forth to a new destiny.

Endings are either the loss of what was or seeds for what will be. It's all up to a person's view of change, and this has powerful implications.

Anxiety, which always accompanies change, can affect your clients in one of two ways. First, if they view change from the negative aspect, it will immobilize them, and they will resist the change. Soon they become like a lifeless, boring, dull, stagnant pond ("Just a trim" again). Second, anxiety can affect your clients in a positive way. ("Just think of the new possibilities I have to create a fresh, exciting new appearance through my stylist!") Not the stagnant pond, but the dancing, exciting ocean. See how important it is to look at change in a positive way?

The anxiety of changing one's image in one case holds back, in the other case is the fuel for change. Anxiety is the possibility of new, positive, springtime beginnings for your clients.

RECOGNIZING CLIENT RESISTANCE TO CHANGE

In general, there are only five reasons a client resists change: (1) Cost: "Prove to me this service is worth it." (2) Companions' approval: "Will my friends, family, or significant people in my life like it?" (3) Concern over whether it will work: "Will this service backfire on me?" (4) Comfort: "Will the new look really be me?" and (5) Questioning self-worth: "Do I really deserve this?"

Resistance 1: Anxiety over Cost. If all of the other client resistances were dealt with, cost would not be an important issue in most instances. In fact, clients often mask one of the other resistances with the question of cost.

Resistance 2: Anxiety over Other People's Approval. The person whose motivation to resist change comes from uncertainty about how others will respond is easy to recognize. In general, she is a person who needs everyone's approval, including your own. This person is a "pleaser" who wants to be liked and is easily influenced by others. You will hear statements like, "I don't know how my husband would feel about my getting a color." She is giving you a clue to her resistance that reveals her anxiety about change. As a stylist, remember anxiety represents a positive possibility. Instead of focusing on the negative component of anxiety, turn it around and help her see the positive side of her statement.

> **Client:** I don't know how my husband would feel about my getting a color.
>
> **Stylist:** He might be excited about it when he sees you! Sounds as if you're excited about it. Have you considered asking him and showing your enthusiasm about a new look?

Resistance 3: Anxiety over Whether the Service Will Work. This client may have had a bad experience in a salon or may have a friend who had a negative one. Reassurance and guarantees are important ways of overcoming this person's resistance to maximizing her appearance by additional services. Reassure her by telling her about new technological breakthroughs in perms and colors or share testimonials from others. Turn the negative anxiety into an anxiety of positive possibility: Just imagine how you will look. Assure her you will use the safest product you have. It's guaranteed. Try not to let a bad experience in her past limit the vision of who she can become.

Resistance 4: Anxiety over Feeling Comfortable with the New Look. "Yes, but I don't know if color in my hair is really me!" expresses an anxiety of becoming someone different. Help this person see that there were many times in her life when growth and change helped her to become a better person.

> **Client:** Yes, but I don't know if color in my hair is really me.

> **Stylist:** Well, there was a time you weren't a school teacher, wasn't there? You graduated from college, and that first day in the classroom, you grew from not being a teacher into being one. It was always in you, in the form of potential. Growing into a new you is just tapping your potential, graduating to a new level in terms of appearance. In less than a week you won't even know your hair is a different color, except through the nice compliments you get when people ask you if you lost weight!

Resistance 5: Anxiety over Whether I Deserve This New Service. In the chapter on Freud, we discussed how a harsh superego (conscience) can cause someone to be her own worst enemy. Such a person lacks feelings of worth and has poor self-esteem. This is the very one who needs the boost of a new look — and a new outlook. You can help her to see that, as well as get her to think not just about herself but also about those around her. Reassure her by turning negative anxiety into positive anxiety: "You surely deserve it.

When is the last time you let yourself go a little?" The sensitive stylist recognizes resistance to change and helps people overcome it — if the stylist feels that, underneath, they are ready and do want to change.

Certain times in life are natural change points. A client is then more ready to change her self-image as reflected by a new hairstyle. These are called *HIGH-READINESS POINTS FOR CHANGE*. There are other times when she is not ready for a new recommendation. These are *LOW-READINESS POINTS FOR CHANGE*.

CLUES TO HIGH AND LOW READINESS FOR CHANGE

The field of Salon Psychology continually stresses the use of High-Touch Empathy to build smooth communications between stylist and client. With open communication, changes in your client's lifestyle, or new experiences or attitudes toward self, are immediately revealed to you. Since hairstyle depends upon lifestyle, new cuts, colors, or perms may be ways of expressing more fully her evolving personality.

Sensitive stylists are in tune with changes in their clients' lives as they occur. High-touch stylists can almost sense when clients are on the verge of such change. In fact, stylists have told me that they saw wedding proposals coming before the clients did!

Consider these three levels of *READINESS FOR CHANGE*, and remember the important role anxiety plays:

Level 1: Low. Here the client is in her comfort zone — contented, fulfilled. At this level she might be annoyed by a stylist who pushes her to change. She worked hard to get here and she wants to enjoy it. She has no anxiety, so there is no motivation for change. And why should there be? If, however, her lifestyle does change, or if she stays at this level too long, she may move to Level 2.

Level 2: Moderate. Something is missing in the client. She is in a rut, bored, unfulfilled, stagnant, stuck. Her fixated self-image finds her aimless, no new possibilities; just get by. She may even be burned out. Perhaps she feels helpless to do anything about it. At this level a stylist-initiated recommendation can be extremely effective because of the client's narrow vision and passivity, from which the stylist can lead her out. The stylist will, of course, be heightening her anxiety level in a positive way by showing her new possibilities which include some risk. At the present time, her anxiety is blocked, and she probably wouldn't have the courage or insight on her own. She could be someone who has had the same job for twenty-two years and has had the same outlook on life for the last thirty years. She is just trying to make it through and feels no excitement.

Level 3: High. Your client is now ready to get out of the rut of Level 2 and "wants to take a chance again." This is the highest-level anxiety point, but motivation for change outweighs anxiety. A change in job or marital status, a new home, a new car, a change in lifestyle, e.g., exercising, losing weight, a promotion, a graduation, a birthday that is significant, a new boyfriend or girlfriend, are all natural clues for the sensitive stylist that this client is at a high readiness for change, a level where motivation exceeds anxiety. The stylist simply reflects her observation of the lifestyle change and talks about new hairstyles that will be congruent with her client's evolving feelings.

At Level 1, the stylist avoids a new recommendation. At Level 2, the stylist actively encourages the client to bring herself into a new perspective. This is the most active level for the stylist because the client's anxiety level exceeds her motivation-for-change level. At Level 3, the stylist doesn't need to actively encourage but can simply facilitate the change since the client's motivation exceeds her anxiety level.

SUMMARY OF CLIENT ANXIETY AND RESISTANCE TO CHANGE

This chapter on change, anxiety, and resistance to change was based upon the writings of the brilliant psychoanalyst, Dr. Rollo May. The Field of Salon Psychology addressed these issues from the salon client's perspective, conscious as well as unconscious.

That anxiety is a necessary, unavoidable part of any change was reiterated. No anxiety, no change; no change, no anxiety. A new view of anxiety was also expressed. Anxiety, a force that makes us tense, butterflyish, nervous, is also the driving force in all positive growth. It is a feeling that whispers to us about new possibilities, new beginnings. Sometimes when we see only the negative side of anxiety, we think about our old "self-image," which we could lose. Positive focusing on anxiety tells us that such endings are really the new beginnings of who we can be.

This chapter also addressed the client's five main resistances to change: (1) anxiety over cost, (2) anxiety over whether her friends will approve, (3) anxiety over whether the service will work properly, (4) anxiety over feeling comfortable with her new self-image, and (5) anxiety over whether she really deserves this new service. The stylist was given ways to help people see the positive side of anxiety and to motivate them to become all they are capable of becoming.

Finally, you were given clues for recognizing high-readiness points for change and low-readiness points for change in the client's life. These provide good, solid ideas for recommending new hairstyles, either actively or passively.

As you have seen, self-image sometimes resists change, even if the change is positive. In the next chapter, a world-renowned plastic surgeon, Dr. Maxwell Maltz, gives his ideas on self-image. His field of psycho-cybernetics shows you how to grow and help your clients reach new goals.

CHAPTER 12

PSYCHO-CYBERNETICS AND SALON GOAL ACHIEVEMENT

THE THEORY OF MAXWELL MALTZ

Maxwell Maltz concluded, "The self-image is the key to human personality and human behavior." Change the self-image, and you change the personality and the behavior. More than this, the self-image sets the boundaries of individual achievement. It defines what you can and cannot do. Expand the self-image, and you expand the area of the possible. The development of an adequate, realistic self-image seems to imbue the individual with new capabilities and new talents. It literally turns failure into success. As a stylist, you can change your client's self-image.

Soon You Will Be Able To:

- Use the power of psycho-cybernetics to achieve your salon goals.

- Help change your clients' future by changing their cosmetic self-image.

- View mistakes as positive because they are simply trial-and-error clues on your road to success.

SELF-IMAGE: THE KEY TO PERSONALITY

One of the most important and creative breakthroughs in the field of psychology was achieved not by a psychologist but by a plastic surgeon, Dr. Maxwell Maltz. Maltz observed the fact that dramatic personality changes sometimes took place after cosmetic surgery. It wasn't too difficult to understand how a woman who was scarred seriously became more outgoing when she was given a new face. Neither was it hard to understand why a teenager with huge ears changed his personality when his ears were surgically reduced in size. These observations didn't particularly interest Maltz, but what did fascinate the surgeon was why didn't other patients, who experienced the same surgery, show personality changes, too? Why did they show no increase in self-confidence and self-esteem? Maltz wrote:

> But what about the exceptions who didn't change? — the duchess who all her life had been terribly shy and self-conscious because of a tremendous bump on her nose. Although surgery gave her a classic nose and a face that was truly beautiful, she still continued to act the part of an ugly duckling, the unwanted sister who could never bring herself to look another human being in the eye. If the scalpel was magic, why did it not work on the duchess?

> Or what about all of the others who acquired a new face but went right on wearing the same old personality? Or how can one explain the reaction of those people who insist that the surgery made no difference whatsoever in their appearance? Every plastic surgeon has had this experience and has probably been as baffled as I was. No

matter how drastic the change in appearance may be, there are certain patients who will insist, "I look just the same as before — you didn't do a thing." Friends, even family, may scarcely recognize them, may become enthusiastic over this newly acquired beauty, yet the patient herself insists that she can see only slight or no improvement, or in fact she denies that any changes have been made.

Maltz discovered that personality changes do not automatically result from cosmetic surgery but are dependent upon something even deeper, and that is the person's self-image. The renowned surgeon started a new career, giving his patients what he called a "spiritual face-lift," helping them remove emotional scars and helping them to change their attitudes and thoughts as well as their physical appearance. The new field of study founded by Maltz was called psycho-cybernetics.

USING THE POWERS OF PSYCHO-CYBERNETICS TO REACH YOUR GOALS

Maltz, like his personal friend Alfred Adler, was very optimistic about the possibilities sleeping inside a human being. They also agreed on another idea. They both felt that people strive for goals and that all behavior is directed by goals — either known and consciously stated or unknown. Every action is steered to achieve something either positive or negative. In fact, the word "cybernetics" means steering mechanism, and thus "psycho-cybernetics" implies that our behavior is steered by our known or unknown goals. According to Maltz:

> Self-image psychology has not only been proved on its own merits, but it explains many phenomena which have long been known but not properly understood in the past. For example, there is today irrefutable clinical evidence in the fields of individual psychology, psycho-somatic medicine, and industrial psychology that there are "success-type personalities" and "failure-type personalities," "happiness-prone personalities" and "unhappiness-prone personalities." Self-image psychology

throws new light on these and on many other observable facts of life. It throws new light on "the power of positive thinking" and, more important, why it works with some people and not with others. (Positive thinking does indeed work when it is consistent with an individual's self-image. It literally cannot work when it is inconsistent with the self-image — until the self-image has been changed.)

The innovative doctor believed that the human brain and nervous system created an elegant and complex "goal-striving" or steering mechanism, a built-in guidance system which, depending upon a person's self-image, either worked for or against him. Like a computer, however, it was powerless until you, the operator, gave it the goal.

The steering mechanism operates by the following principles, according to Maltz:

1. Your built-in steering mechanism must have a target or goal. That goal must be conceived as "already in existence — now," either in actual or potential form. It operates by (1) steering you to a goal already in existence or by (2) "discovering" something already in existence.

2. The automatic mechanism is teleological, that is, operates or must be oriented to "end results," i.e., goals. Do not be discouraged because the "means whereby" may not be apparent. It is the function of the automatic mechanism to supply the means when you supply the goal. Think in terms of end results, and the means will often take care of themselves.

3. Do not be afraid of making mistakes or of temporary failures. All servomechanisms achieve their goals by negative feedback, or by going forward, making mistakes, and immediately correcting course.

4. Skill learning of any kind is accomplished by trial and error, mentally correcting your aim after an error until a successful "motion" — movement or performance — is achieved. After that, further learning and continued success are accomplished by forgetting past errors and remembering successful response so that it can be imitated.

5. You must learn to trust your creative mechanism to do its work and not "jam it" by becoming overly concerned or too anxious as to whether or not it will work. Don't attempt to force it by too much conscious effort. You must "let it work" rather than "make it work." This trust is necessary because the creative mechanism operates below the level of consciousness. You cannot know what is going on beneath the surface. Moreover, it operates spontaneously by nature, according to present need. You have, therefore, no guarantees in advance. It comes into operation as you act and as your actions place a demand upon it. You must not wait to act until you have proof; you must behave as if it were there. It will come through! "Do the thing and you will have the power," said Emerson.

What goals do you have in mind? Don't limit yourself by your past experiences or by others' opinions of you. Dream of some ultimate goal or achievement for yourself. When you let your imagination flow freely, without jamming or blocking your dream goal, plant that goal firmly in mind. Literally "see it" in your mind's eye. Feel it with excitement. Experience it as though you have just reached it. Add rich colors to the picture in your mind. Add sounds, music, or voices. Add people if you like. Vividly imagine the setting by adding other elements. Take a few minutes and return to this page when this concept seems real to you.

Maltz has demonstrated in numerous experiments how the self-image is changed and achievements are made possible not by knowledge but only by actual experiences. And the great news is that one can experience achievements without yet having actually attained them. The mind, itself, can synthetically supply the experience. Maltz explains:

> Experimental and clinical psychologists have proved beyond a shadow of a doubt that the human nervous system cannot tell the difference between an actual experience and an experience imagined vividly and in detail. Although this may appear to be a rather extravagant statement, these synthetic experiences have been used in practical ways to improve skill in dart throwing and shooting basketball goals. They have been

used by individuals to improve their skill in public speaking, overcome fear of the dentist, develop social poise, develop self-confidence, sell more goods — and practically every other conceivable type of situation where "experience" is recognized to bring success.

CHANGING SELF-IMAGE TO CHANGE YOUR FUTURE

Your self-image changes through achieving goals in your professional career. Learning a new style, perm, or color gives you confidence and enhances your own self-image. Often stylists are a little afraid of trying something different for the first time, for example a new type of cut. By remembering Maltz's five points on the steering mechanism, you can perform that new cut "synthetically," experiencing it in your head, doing it over and over in your mind while you are in a relaxed state. Remember, your brain or nervous system cannot tell the difference between a real or a synthetic experience. If you visualize a great, beautiful cut in your mind's eye, your steering mechanism will take you there. You don't even have to pick up shears yet. In your first few synthetic experiences, don't let yourself get jammed, blocked, or frustrated by making mistakes. Simply let your internal guidance system correct them. You will have developed a good cut! When you feel comfortable, pick up the shears. You are ready, filled with confidence from your synthetic practice.

What about encouraging clients to try new services or home-care products? How do you build your self-image and the confidence to do so? Again, simply visualize the end goal. See yourself as a top-notch recommender, one of the best. Forget where you have been. Visualize, with full color and all of your rich senses, a successful recommendation and a happy client. When you have locked-in your goal, take yourself through a few synthetic trips whereby, in your mind, you are experiencing the process of recommending. Don't be alarmed by mistakes or rejection — they are simply clues to a new course. In no time, your brain and your nervous system will have incorporated these new behaviors — a new you, a new self-image, and a new future. Perhaps you might want to read the whole of Maltz's book, *Psycho-Cybernetics*.

SUMMARY

One of the most significant pioneers in psychology was not a psychologist but a plastic surgeon, Dr. Maxwell Maltz. He discovered the importance of a person's self-image to his behavior. Self-image determines success, and it can be developed through experience. The experience can be real, or, just as effective, it can be synthetic (imagined).

Maltz believed that the human being is goal-directed and has a cybernetic steering system operating continuously, even in sleep, to reach its goals. It is vital to have clear goals to steer oneself toward. When mistakes are made in the trial-and-error trip to the goal, they simply indicate a correction in course is necessary. Goal achievement leads to enhanced self-image, which starts to create a winning feeling and has a snowball effect on future successes. Millions of lives have been changed by the innovative idea of psycho-cybernetics.

CHAPTER 13

DESIGNING THE ULTIMATE HIGH-TOUCH SALON ENVIRONMENT

THE THEORY OF B. F. SKINNER

Much has been said about the importance of environment as a cause or determiner of people's behavior. It has been proved that people will tend to repeat actions or behaviors that the environment rewards and will tend to stop those behaviors that are unrewarded. Is it possible that in the salon environment, the human and physical components are so important that they can actually affect whether or not people feel relaxed, purchase retail products, desire a perm or color or new style, or even return? Noted Harvard professor B. F. Skinner, developer of behavioristic psychology and behavior modification, believes that you can condition people through environmental rewards to respond and act in certain ways.

Soon You Will Be Able To:

- Master the principles of behavior modification to assure success with people.

- Understand the importance of reinforcements or rewards on people's behavior.

- Develop a salon environment that gives off warm, positive vibes to people.

Freud talked about the unconscious, Jung discussed the collective unconscious, and Adler and Maltz theorized about a person's underlying self-image as being important in understanding his behavior. B. F. Skinner, the developer of behavioristic psychology, was uninterested in such concepts and would investigate only "behaviors" that could be measured or observed. While Freud might say that a person drinks or smokes excessively because of underlying oral needs, Skinner would only go so far as to say that all we can know is what we measure: She drank three glasses of wine and smoked five cigarettes.

The environment is a place that can be observed, and Skinner noticed that the way an individual responded to the physical and human components of the environment tended to shape that individual's actions in certain ways. This philosophy is a type of "environmental determinism." In Skinner's system, he has no interest in the concept of free will. In fact, one of Skinner's books is entitled *Beyond Freedom and Dignity,* suggesting that people act in ways based not upon their own personal choice but upon the environmental conditioning of their past.

ENVIRONMENTAL VIBES

My kitchen has Mexican tile, and brightly colored Mexican rugs draped over the wooden chairs, and a Mexican umbrella rises from the center of the breakfast table. I have a lot of fun with friends as we sit in the kitchen with some lively Mexican music playing in the background. I ask them where they would like to have dinner that night. As you might expect, somehow or other they seem to be in the mood for Mexican food. (Perhaps by making this paragraph a part of your environment, you are also getting hungry for Mexican food. Without this paragraph's influencing you, chances are Mexican food would not have been on your mind.)

In my living room are dozens of inspiring newspaper clippings of success stories, paintings of mountains and oceans and world changers, plus numerous positive quotes and plaques that are uplifting. When I am sitting in the living room with a friend who is "down and out," I excuse myself for a few minutes and invite the person to feel free to browse. When I come back, I see a more hopeful, cheery person with a more positive perspective. It is always different if the environment gives out good vibes. The physical and "people" part of the environment play an important role in affecting behaviors. How did Skinner first discover this important concept of behavioral psychology?

CONDITIONING PIGEONS

In the 1930s, while Skinner was feeding some pigeons, he discovered something very interesting. He found that whenever he gave a pigeon some food, the pigeon would repeat the exact behavior it was doing at the moment it received its reward or reinforcer. If the pigeon was walking at a forty-five degree angle to the left and was rewarded, it repeated that walk. It wasn't long before the pigeon was being conditioned to walk in figure eights or whatever pattern Skinner wanted from the pigeon.

Skinner started to apply these principles to human behavior, and behavior modification soon became an important part of training in schools, hospitals, and prisons, as well as with athletic teams and sales forces, and even in changing one's own habits. The principle of behavior modification simply states that people will tend to repeat behavior exhibited at the moment of reward. The more immediate the reward or reinforcer to the actual behavior, the more effective it is in causing that behavior to be repeated. The ideal time from behavior to reinforcer should be no longer than a second; otherwise, the behavior that is reinforced and likely to occur again may be another one, one closer to the reinforcement.

EFFECTIVE REINFORCERS

Some reinforcers that can be employed to create the ultimate High-Touch salon include *social, physical or physiological, financial,* and *fear-reducing reinforcers.*

Social reinforcers are the most important for some people who seek out salon services. Social reinforcers include giving time and attention, touching, smiling, calling a person by her name, or complimenting her dress and hair.

Add some social reinforcers of your own:

_____

_____

_____

_____

Physical or physiological reinforcers are rewards that make people feel good in a bodily sense or that fulfill or reduce a physiological need. The primary physiological reinforcer is food. The old idea of the barber handing a child a lollipop was theoretically sound from a behavior-modification perspective! Add physical reinforcers here:

_____

_____

_____

_____

Financial reinforcers are either specials, coupons that a client can use to reduce costs of services or products, free services or products for referring others, or any other monetary reward for desirable behavior. Can you add any other creative ways of applying financial reinforcers?

_____

_____

_____

_____

Fear-reducing reinforcers are those that take away a specific fear that your client has, e.g., fear of a hair color. Fear-reducing reinforcers are called *negative reinforcement* while social, physical or physiological, and financial rewards are called *positive reinforcment*.

Note that both negative and positive reinforcers are rewarding to the client; the one removes a fear, and the other adds incentives. Skinner found punishment, or the applying of a negative consequence after an undesirable behavior, to be very ineffective. Punishment, in fact, creates a need to retreat from the causal situation. Anyone in a stressful salon or anyone who has been exposed to an angry stylist is less likely to return to that punishing environment — especially in the age of High Touch!

USING BEHAVIOR MODIFICATION IN THE SALON

With an understanding of the importance of environmental vibes and behavior reinforcers, let's take a look at the system of behavior modification in action. To modify behavior or to increase the likelihood of having the desired behavior repeated, it is important to do both of these following steps:

STEP 1: *Identify the behavior that is desired.* For example, if a young child is acting responsibly and is not disturbing the salon, simply reinforce the child at some point. Remember the reinforcers. If, however, the child is disruptive, identify a desirable behavior — sitting instead of running — and when the child shows any behavior in the right direction, reinforce it. This is called shaping successive approximations of the desirable behavior.

STEP 2: *Apply an appropriate reinforcer at the exact moment when the desirable behavior occurs or at the moment the behavior to be shaped takes place.* If the behavior desired is for a person to seek out more benefits from the salon, then at the moment she says, "I've been thinking about a perm," the reinforcer needs to be applied. A social reinforcer might be, "With a perm you'd get a lot of compliments"; a physical reinforcer might be, "You'd feel great"; a financial reinforcer could be, "And today our perms are on special"; a fear-reducing reinforcer could be, "We have a great, safe product that is specially designed for perming your bleached hair."

Again, it is most important in setting up your High-Touch salon environment that you identify desirable behaviors and reward them when they occur.

DESIGNING THE ULTIMATE HIGH-TOUCH SALON ENVIRONMENT

Your salon can apply the principles of behavior modification at every step along the way in the client's salon experience. In Chapter 3, "Amazing People with Your Sensitivity to Service," nine key service points in your client's passage through the salon were identified. How can reinforcers be provided at a few of these points to increase the probability of the client's feeling comfortable?

1. Salon Contact: When the client calls for an appointment, that is a desirable behavior. Do we want to see that behavior occur again in the future? Of course. So what type of reinforcer can you build into that salon contact? (Remember the four types of reinforcers.)

_____

_____

_____

_____

2. Client Walks into Salon: Certainly it is desirable behavior when a client enters our salon for service or for products, so it needs to be reinforced immediately. What are some ways you can do this?

_____

_____

_____

_____

_____

3. Client Consultation: Is it a desirable behavior when a client asks for a consultation? Certainly. Again, create some ways of reinforcing the consultation, including additional services, benefits, and products.

_____

_____

_____

_____

4. Completion of Services: List some reinforcers.

_____

_____

_____

_____

5. Purchase of Hair-Care Products: Create some reinforcers for their selection.

_____

_____

_____

_____

6. Payment for Services: How can this be reinforced?

_____

_____

_____

_____

7. Rebooking: How can we respond to a rebooking by using behavior modification?

_____

_____

_____

_____

It is very important in designing the ultimate High-Touch salon environment that we consider the role of colors and music plus the social mood as effective reinforcement in the salon environment. When you synergistically bring together the human and physical environment plus good High-Tech Designing, you give clients the ultimate experience. They won't ask for Mexican food, but they will ask for a rebooking!

SUMMARY OF DESIGNING THE ULTIMATE HIGH-TOUCH SALON ENVIRONMENT

Behavior modification is a system of psychology developed by B. F. Skinner in which specific desirable behaviors are identified and immediately reinforced. In those instances when desirable behaviors are not exhibited, it is necessary to reinforce or shape behaviors that are in the desired direction. Positive reinforcers may be social, physical or physiological, and financial. Negative reinforcers reduce or remove fear. Finally, punishment, applying a noxious or painful stimulus after an undesirable behavior, is the least effective influence on people.

Skinner emphasized the importance of environmental reinforcers on behavior, and this chapter was designed to help you think about ways to make your salon environment the ultimate High-Touch place for your clients today. You have as much control over your environment as your environment has over you. So why not build the best?

CHAPTER 14

SOARING OVER SALON STRESS THROUGH RATIONAL THINKING

THE THEORY OF ALBERT ELLIS

Albert Ellis tells us that events in our lives don't disturb and stress us, but what does is the way we look at these events. Why is it that two people who face the same stressful experience in life may respond differently? It's because of the way each thinks about it. Rational thinking can ultimately make us more capable of soaring over salon stress.

Soon You Will Be Able To:

- Understand why some people in the salon "blow up" at the slightest incident while others can handle almost anything.

- Identify the four major ways to look at life that cause unhappiness, and find your new outlooks for happiness.

- Use the mental powers of rational thinking to help you deal more effectively with stress, pressure, and setbacks.

SOARING OVER STRESS THROUGH RATIONAL THINKING

You have no doubt heard the phrase, "You are what you eat." But are you aware that you also are what you think? Yes, perhaps the most powerful psychological revelation of the century is that your thinking affects your emotions, which in turn affect your actions. Behavioral research and clinical experiences accumulate more evidence each day to show the relationships between your thinking and your depressions, anxieties, fears, guilt, temper and anger-related problems, feelings of failure and inferiority, and even unhappiness or dissatisfaction in life. Bad or irrational thoughts really can cause stress in many ways.

The great news is that just as you can be master of your diet, so can you achieve mastery over your thoughts, which will help you live life more positively. This chapter, based upon the ideas and research of Albert Ellis, shows how you can rid yourself of emotional problems and win happiness and success by using the powerful artillery of Rational Thinking, the greatest human weapon against unhappiness.

Consider these stylists facing typical salon stressers:

Betty gets all upset and flies off the handle when a client is late; Vicky finds some things to do as she waits for her client to arrive. Both Betty and Vicky are experiencing the same situation, yet one is devastated by it and ruins her own (and others') day. The other accepts it and finds new ways to be productive.

Jim gets hurt and sulks when a client expresses dissatisfaction with a cut; Eddie thanks the client for the feedback and does something to help her be satisfied. Again, although both of them are experiencing the same situation, for one it is stressful while for the other it is productive.

Why are Betty and Jim less able to handle stress than Vicky and Eddie? Were they born that way? No, says Dr. Albert Ellis, a stimulating modern-day psychologist who, with Dr. Robert Harper, wrote *A New Guide to Rational Living*. Betty and Jim are simply looking at the situation irrationally, while Vicky and Eddie are Rational Thinkers.

How does this important idea and skill of Rational Thinking work?

BECOMING A RATIONAL THINKER: IT'S AS EASY AS A-B-C!

The irrational thinker faces a situation helplessly with a tendency to catastrophize. The rational thinker faces the same situation with a plan either to accept it, change it, or turn that situation into an even better outcome. Ellis has demonstrated very clearly how our emotions develop — positive ones like joy, happiness, or contentment, and negative ones like anger, fear, or hurt. The New York City psychologist illustrated the development of emotions by using an A-B-C analogy.

At "A" in our life is some Activating Event. An Activating Event occurs when something happens that Activates the mind to create an emotional reaction. For example, when Betty's client doesn't show up on time, that Activated Betty's mind to create a reaction, to think about it or talk to herself about it. When Jim's client said she didn't like the cut, that Activated Jim's mind to form a reaction. After the Activating Event occurs, then "B" is the next step in how positive or negative emotions form.

At "B" we establish a Belief about the Activating Event. We do so by either thinking about it, talking to ourselves about it, or, even worse, doing neither and just letting our emotions run away without being rational at all. Betty probably told herself, "That so-and-so client makes me so angry I could lose it. Why does she have to be so inconsiderate? I'm boiling.

She should be here. This is the third time, and I can't stand it!"

Now take a moment and read those thoughts to yourself a few times. After you are finished, jot down how you feel and what kinds of emotions you are experiencing.

_____

_____

_____

_____

Next, use the same situation and consider the other stylist, Vicky, and the Belief that she takes toward "A" (the late client), the Activating Event. Create an imaginary dialogue between Betty and Vicky.

_____

_____

_____

_____

Did your dialogue read something like this?

Betty: That client makes me angry!

Vicky: She can't make you angry. Only you can make you angry because of the way you look at it. If you are angry, you haven't found the most productive way of looking at the situation.

Betty: I'm boiling. She should be here!

Vicky: No, she shouldn't be here.

Betty: Why shouldn't she be here?

Vicky: Because she's not here! She's somewhere else. Isn't it only rational that regardless of whether you think she should or should not be here, she isn't?

Betty: Well, I just can't stand it!

Vicky: Sure you can, Betty. You can stand it. You know how I know? I know because you are standing it!

Vicky's reaction to the late client: "I wish she had been on time because it would certainly have been better and more convenient for me. But she's not on time, and I will have to accept that. I'll talk to her about it next time. And while I wait, let me call a few people who tried new services recently and find out how they liked their new styles. I'm especially interested in talking to Davis, who tried a perm."

Now take a few seconds to get into Vicky's world. Reread her Beliefs about the situation in the last paragraph and jot down some of the emotions you now experience.

_____

_____

_____

_____

_____

Did you have different emotions to the same situations based upon whose Beliefs you made part of you? Whatever your emotions were, that is the "C" part of how events lead to beliefs which lead to emotions A-B-C.

The "C" in your life is the Consequent Emotion that you will experience.

If you compare the two sides of this chart, irrational and rational beliefs, you can predict your emotions at "C".

Irrational Beliefs	**Rational Beliefs**
Things should go my way.	Things are the way they are! What is, is!
The world should make it easier on me. I shouldn't get too many inconveniences, like traffic jams, late clients, broken-down washing	Earth is to its galaxy as one grain of sand is to a beach. I, one person among five billion, am just as insignificant. How could the world possi-

machines and driers, no parking spaces, and sometimes crabby clients.

bly be arranged around me and my conveniences? Traffic jams have nothing to do with me — they are just the result of people like me on their way to work.

In a way, I am creating this jam by being here! And broken-down washers and driers in the salon don't happen because of me — they happen because some parts are malfunctioning. In fact, I was part of the reason for their malfunctioning! That there are no parking spaces tells me that all of these selfish people who came in earlier than I did decided to take the most convenient spaces instead of leaving one for me! I certainly would have left a close space for them if I'd come early. Sure I would!

There's just nothing I can do about this situation I'm in!

If there's nothing I can do about the situation I am in, then I don't have to do anything! So I'll take my mental and physical energies and get other things done.

I'm worried about everything.

Worrying never helps. Do your best to deal with problems when they arise instead of burning up the moment with worrying

	about events in the future, which in most cases never even occur.
I can't stand it!	Not only can I stand it, but I'm going to get stronger from it. I'm going to turn this event into one of the best outcomes possible. I can!

It's like A-B-C. When an Activating Event happens to you in the salon or at home, remember this chapter and *determine to build your mental muscle at "B."* Rationally develop the best belief about the event. Talk to yourself rationally. Your reward? A healthy, happy emotional self who takes pride in coping with stress. You will be like Vicky and Eddie!

Albert Ellis identified a number of irrational thoughts or beliefs about life that are the biggest causes of stress.

FOUR IRRATIONAL BELIEFS THAT CAUSE STRESS

Remember, it's the way you look at an Activating Event — rationally or irrationally — that ultimately determines the Consequent Emotions you experience. What power to soar over salon stress! Here are the four common areas of irrational thinking that all of us use at times and how to win control over self-defeating emotions with rational thoughts.

Memorize the four rational ideas to use at "B" in the A-B-C System.

Irrational Idea 1

I must be totally perfect, competent, and achieving in everything I do, so I will never do anything unless I know it will be perfect ahead of time. Unless I'm perfect, I'm worthless.

Rational Idea 1

While I would like to be perfect, would prefer to be perfect, *I don't need to be perfect!* I'll try my best; I'll make mistakes and simply correct them.

Irrational Idea 2

I must be loved and approved by everyone else in the world. I direly need you to OK me in order to be OK.

Rational Idea 2

While I would like everyone to love me and approve of me, I don't need the approval of everyone.

Irrational Idea 3

The world must be just and fair according to my standards. I need justice.

Rational Idea 3

While I am working hard to make a just and fair world and I WANT a just and fair world, I don't need it!

Irrational Idea 4

Events in the world must go in a way that makes life easiest for me; then I can be happy.

Rational Idea 4

While I would like events in the world to go my way, I can stand it if they don't. It's not a matter of life or death. I want it, but I don't need everything to go my way in order for me to be happy!

Whenever you are upset about something in life, chances are you believe one of these four irrational thoughts. Make your thoughts rational. Remember, to want something is rational but to direly need it is irrational.

SUMMARY OF SOARING OVER SALON STRESS THROUGH RATIONAL THINKING

Notice all the stress that can be saved by a clean, rational view of life? Remember the A-B-C's and your power in the way you look at things, either rationally or irrationally. Rational Thinking coupled with your own unlimited, creative ways of coping with any situation places you in a position stronger than the mountain and the ocean. They just respond helplessly to the winds, the moon, the tides, and gravity. You don't have to respond helplessly. By using Rational Thinking, you are creating new possibilities, new emotions, and a new you!

CHAPTER 15

BECOMING AN ENCOURAGING HAIRSTYLIST

THE THEORY OF LEWIS LOSONCY

"Encouragement is first, helping people see all they have going for them; second, helping people create new visions and images of who they could be; and third, and most important, helping them develop the *courage* to become that new vision."

Isn't fear a big factor holding back your client's willingness to improve her style? Isn't the antidote to fear . . . courage? *En-courage-ment* is the process of bringing out your client's courage to overcome fear of change. *Perhaps, Encourage-ment Is the Ultimate Gift of the Professional Cosmetologist!*

Soon You Will Be Able To:

- Identify signs of discouraged clients.

- Make use of the encouragement process to lift clients' appearances and spirits.

- Know how to give your clients the greatest gift of all — the gift of encouragement.

ENCOURAGEMENT, THE ULTIMATE GIFT OF THE PROFESSIONAL COSMETOLOGIST

In every group of people there are always a few who have a positive effect on others. You know them. They are easy to be with, are interested in others, and have a positive view of life and its possibilities. They always have their senses tuned in to better ways. Because of their special attitudes and talents, they have the biggest impact on people. In *The Encouragement Book,* Don Dinkmeyer and Lewis Losoncy called these special people "Encouragers."

The philosopher Teilhard de Chardin said, "The future is in the hands of those who can give tomorrow's generations valid reasons to hope and live." That is exactly what encouragers do. They give courage! Perhaps encouragement, in that sense, is a gift as great as love, but at the least it is a key ingredient in any personal or professional relationship.

Robert White, the Harvard University personality theorist, believes that encouragement is the most significant factor involved in any personality or behavior change. Raymond Corsini, author and educator, asserts that the only enemy to personal growth is fear and that the antidote to fear is courage. The key goal of encouragement is to stimulate someone's courage. Jerome Frank has shown that persuasiveness is the most important attribute for successfully influencing another.

Encouragement is persuasiveness, and is the most effective way to stimulate movement in others and to increase their feelings of worth and their determination to improve. The average cosmetologist has studied and practiced for hundreds and hundreds of hours to refine her technical skills in cutting, coloring, and perming. Yet very little schooling has been given her on how to be an *Encouraging Hairstylist*, the key to professional — and personal — success!

The Encouraging Hairstylist sees the role of client courage in her client's hairstyle change. Consider how important courage is.

COURAGE: THE MAJOR FACTOR THAT DETERMINES WHETHER PEOPLE ACTUALIZE THEIR POTENTIAL

Finish this sentence: With a little more courage, I would

_____.

However you responded, I'd like to suggest to you that your answer is probably very important to you. And look at the only thing keeping you back from achieving your valuable goal — lack of courage!

Winston Churchill said, "Courage is rightly esteemed the first of all human qualities because courage is the quality that guarantees all others." David Seabury showed us that courage is not something mystical but a very practical quality. Seabury expressed the development of courage this way, "We learn courageous action by going forward whenever fear urges us backward." A little boy was once asked how he learned to skate. "Oh, by getting up each time I fell," he responded.

Rudolf Dreikurs, the psychiatrist of common sense, showed us the power of courage. Dreikurs asserted, "Fear is very often not caused by real dangers; even death loses its terror for those who have developed courage." Thomas Carlyle acknowledged the self-fulfilling influence of courage: "Tell people they are courageous and then watch them become more so."

Don Dinkmeyer showed us how a courageous person sees the potential threat of a changing situation. "The courageous person can look at a situation, a task, or an event in terms of possible actions and solutions rather than potential threats and dangers. Therefore, he can move without hesitation, persist without slackening, and proceed without withdrawing."

And Alfred Adler wrote, "Do not forget the most important fact that it is not heredity and it is not environment that are the ultimate determiners of our lives: They are only the building blocks or the raw material out of which we either fearfully or courageously construct the person we are going to be."

The more one studies the importance of courage, the more one realizes that no positive change would ever be resisted if a person had courage. Courage is what keeps your clients in tune. Encouragement is your major non-haircutting tool as a hairstylist!

From Discouragement To Encouragement Through You, The Encouraging Stylist!

The Discouraged Person	The Encouraged Person
1. Seeks sameness: Just a trim or the usual.	1. I'm ready for a new look!
2. Liability focused: My hair is horrible.	2. Asset focused: Well, I think you're right; my hair does have some bounce — maybe a new color would add excitement.
3. Fear: I don't know how I'd look with a perm.	3. Courage: I'll never find out how I could look my best until I explore new possibilities.
4. Low goals: I'm happy, I guess, with my hair the way it is.	4. Expanded goals: As my stylist, what are some new ideas for my hair that you might suggest?
5. Closed-mindedness: I've always worn my hair this way.	5. Open-mindedness to new ways: I want to look different.

The "dis-couraged" person is only one step away from looking the best she could — that one step is courage. That one step is best taken with *The Encouraging Hairstylist!*

WHAT IS ENCOURAGING HAIRSTYLING?

Encouraging Hairstyling (EH) is a positive and practical approach to developing confident and courageous clients. The main belief behind EH is that ultimately people change their hairstyle when they themselves are motivated to change. The primary task in EH is to encourage the client's own willingness and determination to change. The raw material for EH is already there in the client in the form of her assets, resources, and potential of her hair. It is also there in her desire to look the best she possibly can. A new look encouraged by a new outlook, a rearrangement of how she views her possibilities, is what is needed. This is best achieved in the context of an encouraging relationship.

The Encouraging Hairstylist helps the client by first showing her what she already has going for her, then by helping her see visions and images of who she can be. Finally and most important, she helps the client develop the courage to become all that she can be.

THE ENCOURAGEMENT HAIRSTYLING PROCESS

STEP 1: *Identify Some Positive Assets, Strengths, and Resources for Potential in Your Client's Hair.* Make your client a winner, not a loser. An encouraging relationship is one based upon the positive. Remember, whatever you tell someone about her hair, you are telling her about herself! Always start off on a positive note, and if some negative element of the hair has to be addressed, make it a minor afterthought. Speak of it in terms of how you can improve it. Speak of potential, and tie in with her lifestyle. Keep it upbeat and positive; and show her you respect her hair, which means you respect her!

STEP 2: *Help People Create Visions and Images of Who They Can Be.* Clients are tops in your eyes! You care about their looking their best; you understand them and they trust you. Take three sheets of paper; on one put *possible styles*, on one put *possible colors*, and on a third put *possible curls*. Under each, creatively list all of the service possibilities that you can give professionally to every client. With her in your chair, share some new dreams, visions, and images that she can try. The more cuts you show, the more panoramic vistas you open up for your client. Let her see the full rainbow of colors; let her feel the full bounce of the perms. But mainly let her feel the caring behind your creative sharing. Constantly keep tying in the lifestyles of your clients. When you talk about things you took the time to remember about them, you are giving to each of them the ultimate gift of uniqueness and to yourself a feeling of importance. When you see your client's eyes flash in response to a certain vision or appearance, move on to the most important step of EH.

STEP 3: *Help the Client Develop the Courage to Become All That She Can Become.* The client is special in your eyes, and you care. You have explored many new possible images with her, and she has responded to one. The only thing holding her back is . . . COURAGE. Your encouragement makes the difference. Some practical ways to encourage her include: (1) helping her imagine the new look in her mind; (2) making it easy for her to see that the change is not so drastic if it really isn't; (3) helping her see how this new look is more advantageous than the current one; (4) putting the new hairstyle in the context of a new dress, a new skirt, earrings, etc.; (5) offering guarantees when relevant; (6) referring to testimonials or previous clients' experiences with this specific look; (7) discussing some significant others in her life and how they will respond positively; (8) making her enthusiastic not only with the new look but with the new "total person"; (9) helping her feel your excitement about doing the new service for her. Feel free to add any of your own ideas on how to do *Encouraging Hairstyling:*

_____

_____

_____

_____

_____

Remember, *To be the encouraging hairstylist, it is vital to compliment people and have the same enthusiasm after the service as you did before.* If your whole salon is built on being *an encouraging salon team*, what an experience for a client to have — everyone supporting and encouraging the new look, the new person.

SUMMARY OF THE ENCOURAGING HAIRSTYLIST

Courage may very well be the most important quality that a human being can have. With courage, one moves forward in life to find actualization. *The Encouraging Hairstylist* is one who sees the client in the chair, resisting becoming all that she is capable of becoming, as simply lacking courage. *The Encouraging Hairstylist* communicates respect for her and shows caring for her as she is. The stylist helps her create visions of who she can be by identifying all of the potential services that the salon offers. Finally and most important, the stylist *Encourages* the client to actualize her potential and *go for it!*

Can You Think of a Greater Gift?

PART III

BEING SUCCESSFUL WITH ALL DIFFERENT PERSONALITIES THROUGH SALON PSYCHOLOGY

CHAPTER 16

RELAXING
THE SALON
PHOBIC

The salon phobic has a fear of some element of the salon
experience. By understanding this person's scary feelings,
you can give him or her a strong sense of security in your
presence and help your client for a lifetime.

Soon You Will Be Able To:

- Recognize a person who has a salon phobia.

- Understand how a salon phobic views the salon experience.

- Relax a salon phobic to help her overcome what could be a traumatic experience.

Linda was a quiet twenty-nine-year-old housewife who dreaded going to the salon because she was afraid of being noticed or having her name called out in front of others in the reception area. She sought out a few different salons until she found a receptionist who sensed her need to be inconspicuous. In this sensitive salon she didn't feel people were breathing down her neck. The receptionist even started booking Linda when there wasn't a lot of traffic in the salon. She was given a stylist with a personality handpicked for her — a quiet, sensitive, and understanding stylist. These salon professionals assured themselves of not losing this client.

Roy was a Pennsylvania steelman whose barber passed away. He had to find a new place to get a cut. His wife talked him into going to her salon. Sitting in the all-female reception area, seeing heads under dryers, and not seeing any male staff caused the big man to shrink into his chair. He couldn't wait to get out of that intimidating situation.

Louisa was OK in the salon until the cut was over. She feared the moment when her stylist would turn her chair around, make her look into the mirror, and ask in front of everyone else, "What do you think?" It was like a splash of cold water on Louisa's face on a cold day! She couldn't even look at herself because she was imagining that everyone else was looking at her, too. So she just quickly smiled and mumbled a quick, "Good, thanks. I gotta go now!"

Betsy feared that she would trip and make a fool of herself while walking back to the shampooing area.

Jane felt intimidated by her stylist, who was tall, overbearing, and domineering.

Margaret had had her long, beautiful hair cut off once before when she was a model and felt almost nude without it;

finally it had grown back. She was afraid the stylist "wouldn't hear her" when she said "just a half inch off."

Deidre feared the "germs and dirt" in the hair left on her chair from a previous client. She was concerned about the germs on the shears and combs the stylists were using. "Are they really sterilized well enough?" she wondered.

All of these people have something in common. They are suffering from some form of salon phobia. They are not alone. About one in five potential salon clients has this common problem. The great news is that a sensitive staff, by understanding salon phobia, can create an environment that will attract and keep these very special humans who just have a problem with some element of the salon experience.

Add some additional phobias that clients might have as they come to the salon, e.g., cost phobia:

_____

_____

_____

_____

_____

What are the characteristics of salon phobics, and how can we design our salon to relate to them most effectively and win them over as clients?

CHARACTERISTICS OF SALON PHOBICS

A phobia is a fear of some object or situation which presents no actual danger or one in which the danger is magnified out of proportion to its actual seriousness. More specifically for our purposes, the salon phobic is "a person who has a fear about some object, person, or situation in the salon experience." There are some common fears, already named by psychologists, that can relate to the the salon phobic. Ochlophobia is a fear of crowds, as with our client Linda, who dreaded waiting with other people. Another common one is mysophobia, fear of contamination or germs, which our client Deidre experienced. Claustrophobia, fear of closed places, can cause salon clients to seek out large, airy, windowed salons. These phobias are suffered by the general public as well as by salon clients.

There are, however, phobias that pertain just to salons. One of the most common is a phobia related to a severe alteration of appearance through cutting or chemical services. Margaret, is a perfect example. Previous negative experiences and poor stylist-client communications were most likely the causes of this type of phobic reaction.

The fear of being singled out, the phobia our client Linda had, is often found in very self-conscious people. They fear everything from having the focus on themselves at their birthday parties to standing in front of a group of people for whom they are the center of attention. This phobia may be so real that dizziness, sweating palms, and rapid heartbeat will occur. In severe instances a person may experience an anxiety attack.

How is salon phobia developed? How can the salon phobic be made to feel comfortable? What would the personality theorists from Part II say about salon phobics?

FREUDIAN PSYCHOANALYTIC VIEW OF THE SALON PHOBIC

Freud, as you will recall, emphasized the importance of the unconscious in behavior. Thus Freud believed that phobias are "symbolic substitutes" of the real, underlying fear. The phobia is not the real thing but *represents* a real fear. The "real fear" lies in the unconscious conflict between the impulses of the id potentially gaining control and overwhelming the blocking forces of the superego (conscience).

For example, the fear of crowds (ochlophobia) comes from the fear of losing control and acting out the aggression of the id. By avoiding crowds, one doesn't have to face that potentially embarrassing situation. The fear of germs and dirt is an obsession of the superego's striving for cleanliness against any form of dirt — symbolic of the body's waste products, which were regarded as "dirty" in the toilet-training period. That is why some people have a panic attack when they see hair on the chair or when their hands get a little dirty. This ordinarily wouldn't cause distress in most people, but the mysophobic loses control over it. The fear of shears and cutting, Freud would say, was a reflection of the fear of losing one's sexuality through castration or cutting. The fear of having too much hair cut off may represent a fear of losing one's masculinity or femininity.

The important point to remember about psychoanalytic theory is that a phobia represents something deep in the person's unconscious. Thus attempts just to reassure or to deal with surface fears without fully understanding the roles of the id, ego, and superego in their unconscious struggle would be futile. The Freudian view is relevant in the following instances with salon phobics:

1. You have tried everything, but the client still has phobias, anxiety symptoms, or traumas.

2. The person can't explain why she feels the way she does, but she is anxious about something.

3. There appears no logical, rational, conscious reason for the fear.

4. The individual has never had a bad experience in the salon.

Considering their symbolic importance, there are many preventive approaches to minimize the impact of phobias that spring from unconscious sources. Here are some practical suggestions, using the psychoanalytic model, for helping the salon phobic feel more comfortable:

1. Recognize the importance of a clean, sterile salon. If, for some of your clients, dirt is symbolic of the body's waste products at an unconscious level, make sure that the salon is as clean as possible. This includes the rest rooms, visible proof of a sterilized comb, no hair on the floor or chair, and, of course, a stylist who is clean.

2. To minimize the trauma of a child's cut and the child's fear of shears, it is ideal to match the three-to-six-year-old child with a stylist of the opposite sex. The little boy, whose first love is Mommy (sometimes his second love is his stylist), feels safer with females. The little girl of the same age feels safer with males. And from six to eleven, just the opposite is true. Here the ideal matching, if possible, is with a stylist of the same sex.

3. Be a safe, reassuring, nonthreatening person. Remember the salon phobics tend to have harsh superegos; they are their own worst enemies and need to be relaxed.

4. If they seem to shrink when you turn them toward the mirror after the cut, avoid doing it the next time.

5. When salon phobics call, they may ask for a time when not many people are in. Reassure them that you understand and will do your absolute best.

6. If possible, match a salon phobic with a quiet, soft-spoken, sensitive stylist.

7. Salon phobics prefer protected, private styling stations.

8. Be cautious about taking them around and introducing them to everyone on their first visit. Give them time to warm up.

B.F. SKINNER AND A BEHAVIORISTIC VIEW OF THE SALON PHOBIC

While psychoanalysts believe that phobias are symbolic of deeper, unconscious fears, behaviorists believe that the phobias themselves are the only things you need to address. They are not considered symbolic of anything else. If someone has a phobia, it is simply because the person has previously had a bad experience in that environment. Indeed, the behavioristic explanation is even more relevant than the psychoanalytic and is, in most instances, a better explanation for the source of salon phobia.

The key idea to remember, according to Skinner, is that *all phobias are learned . . . and can be unlearned!* They were learned through a negative experience in a particular environment and can be unlearned by a positive experience in a similar one. On an everyday level, the child who was thrown into the water to learn how to swim may develop a phobia about water. Someone who went through the experience of being bitten by a dog may develop a phobia about dogs.

The salon phobics are no different. Something about a salon visit unconsciously reminds them of negative experiences in the past.

1. The client who is afraid of crowds may have experienced embarrassing social situations in the past and doesn't want to face that again. Perhaps she fears that if asked a question, she won't know the answer. Under extreme phobic stress, people can even forget their names. So if she does come to the salon, this client will bury her face in a book so she won't risk doing the wrong thing.

2. The child who is afraid of shears has either cut herself, or Mom and Dad have lectured sternly about scissors. The child's experience has caused her to see danger in sharp objects. From a behaviorist's point of view, then, the phobia was, simply, learned.

3. The person afraid of having too much hair taken off or of having a service fail or of having her appearance altered too much has simply had a similar negative experience in the past or was told about one in a way that made a severe impression. Again, the phobia was learned.

4. Someone who has a phobia for cleanliness may have experienced illness or disease in earlier years or perhaps has studied biology or chemistry and has experienced an overemphasis on the importance of sterile environments. Her mind literally pictures all sorts of germs growing.

Get the picture? See how differently behaviorists and psychoanalysts view phobias? It is important to understand both views to be most effective.

Remember, behaviorists believe that salon phobias are learned . . . and can be unlearned. How important it is to build a plan to help phobics feel comfortable, considering the huge numbers of phobics. Use these practical suggestions to help the salon phobic overcome phobia by using behavioristic approaches:

1. Have the receptionist tuned in to recognizing a potential salon phobic over the phone. If she conveys a soft-spoken, sensitive manner and reassures the client that she will be with a sensitive, understanding stylist, it enhances the chances of having the client show up.

2. When speaking to a salon phobic in the reception area, walk over to her rather than call across the room, thus drawing everyone's attention.

3. Accompany the salon phobic to the shampooing area.

4. Dr. Joseph Wolpe, the world's top authority on phobias, recognizes that it is impossible to be both tense and relaxed at the same time. Therefore, give the client a relaxing shampoo. Some salons start by using massage with phobic people to help rid them of some of the anxiety.

5. When giving a frightened child a haircut, comb the hair first, without even picking up the shears. If possible, give a reinforcer (a reward) to the child when you are ready to cut. The reinforcer may be a smile, a touch, candy or food, or a toy. Remember, a behavior that is rewarded will be repeated.

SUMMARY OF THE SALON PHOBIC

A sizable portion of the public experiences salon phobia — or a fear of some element of the salon. Salons lose tens of thousands of clients each year because of not having a plan to deal with them. Millions of others never come at all because of salon phobia. This chapter discussed two major theories of why salon phobia develops and how to help phobics overcome their fear.

The psychoanalytic view, developed by Sigmund Freud, saw phobias as "symbolic substitutes" for real underlying fears which exist in the unconscious struggle between the id, ego, and superego. B. F. Skinner's behavioristic view was that understanding phobias was much simpler. Phobias were learned in response to negative experiences . . . and could be unlearned in new positive ones.

There are thousands of potential clients out there in the world, salon phobics who are waiting for that special stylist. Why can't it be you?

CHAPTER 17

CONDITIONING THE ATTENTION-SEEKING CLIENT

Whether using "pity me" or bragging, attention seekers often elicit irritating emotions in the stylist. How can you deal most effectively with the attention seeker?

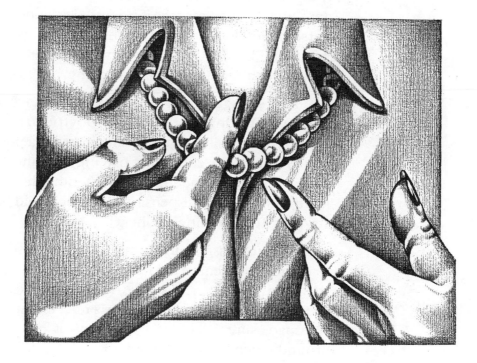

Soon You Will Be Able To:

- Know why some people in the salon need so much attention.

- Recognize all of the different forms of attention-seeking behaviors, from "pity me" to "notice me."

- Cope more effectively with attention seekers.

Jean was a sad sack. The homely teenager spoke very little, but unhappiness could be heard beneath her silence. Everyone on the salon staff pitied her and did whatever she could to pick her up. Nothing seemed to give Jean a lift. Her stylist once gave her a free cut and products for her hair. That didn't help. The receptionist even tried to fix her up with Michael, another client, for a blind date. Jean said, "No, he probably wouldn't like somebody like me." No one could think of anything more to do.

Sarah was, to say the least, a real downer of a client. Every Wednesday at 10:45 she'd arrive, complaining about one thing or another. She never had a good word to say about anything. It was almost as if a cloud descended on the four-person salon for the hour that the forty-five-year-old woman was there. Even after she won the lottery, all she said was, "Yeah, but after taxes I'll have nothing."

Cheryl's bragging was a constant annoyance to the staff. If she wasn't talking about all of her boyfriends, it was all her new clothes or all the money she makes as a photographer. It was as if she were constantly playing the game "Can You Top This?" with everyone she met. Sometimes her stylist had to leave and go to the dispensary to get her head back on straight after listening to Cheryl.

Jim, a businessman in his mid-forties, was starting to become a problem to the female stylists. He constantly asked them out, and in one instance, made advances to one of them. He got angry when the girls rejected him, and everyone made sure that there were always at least two people around when Jim was in the salon.

Helen was a regular for years, but ever since her retirement she was becoming more and more annoying to the staff. She got extremely touchy if she had to wait past her appointment time and constantly told the receptionists, "I'm a busy woman. I don't have all day. I've got a lot of things going on in my life."

All of these salon clients, Jean, Sarah, Cheryl, Jim, and Helen have something in common . . . they are all attention seekers. How can you spot them?

THE CHARACTERISTICS OF
ATTENTION-SEEKING CLIENTS

Remembering Albert Adler, we know that attention seekers use many behaviors and emotions to get themselves noticed. Because we are social creatures, all of us need attention from others, but attention seekers have an excessive need for it. They continue to use whichever behaviors or emotions work best to get it for them. The behaviors they "select" become part of their lifestyle. Consider our five attention seeking friends.

Jean uses a "pity-me" approach toward life to invite sympathy. Sarah seeks attention with her attitude of "Look how hard my life is — everything is against me." Cheryl tries to get attention by communicating, "I'm more important than you are. I have more than you do." Jim is seeking attention to reassure himself that he is worthwhile in the eyes of women. And Helen, after a busy, productive career, now lives a slowed-down life that appears empty in relation to her past. She feels in her "private logic" that the staff thinks she has nothing going on in her world, so it doesn't matter if she is the one kept waiting.

COPING WITH ATTENTION-SEEKING CLIENTS
FROM AN ADLERIAN PERSPECTIVE

The attention-seeking client is, perhaps, easiest to deal with if understood accurately by the stylist — easy because you know she is driven by a need for attention, and something can be done about it. But often the attention seeker is misunderstood and is handled by a stylist in a way that further encourages that kind of behavior.

Alfred Adler saw people as socially rooted, their behaviors geared toward fulfilling their needs for attention, recognition, contributing, and belonging. When these needs aren't fulfilled, discouragement may occur; and the individual uses inappropriate behavior and emotions to get those needs met.

Some signs of discouragement include rebellion, sympathy seeking, constant need to be center stage, withdrawal, jealousy of others who are receiving attention, and bragging in a misguided attempt to get respect. The discouraged behavior they select is the one that their "private logic" thinks will be most effective.

Jean's lifestyle of "Pity me; I'm so helpless" is a very effective way of eliciting attention from others. Perhaps this worked very well in getting her mother and father to take responsibility for making her happy. It's working, as well, with the salon staff, who are giving her free haircuts and products. This further reinforces her down-and-out attitude.

Adler would suggest that you not take responsibility for making other people happy. We don't help them by doing so; it only further rewards the down-and-out behavior as a way of getting attention. Instead, give attention to the positive things the client says. In other words, ignore the negative and build on even the smallest positive. Soon, Jean will learn that she gets more attention by being positive than by being negative.

Take some time to develop a strategy for dealing with each of the five salon attention seekers. Feel free to refer again to Adler in Chapter 9 and brush up on your approach. What might you say to each of these?

Jean: _____

_____

_____

_____

_____

Sarah: _____

_____

_____

_____

_____

_____

Cheryl: _____

_____

_____

_____

_____

_____

Jim: _____

_____

_____

_____

_____

_____

Helen: _____

_____

_____

_____

_____

_____

COPING WITH ATTENTION-SEEKING CLIENTS FROM SKINNER'S BEHAVIOR-MODIFICATION APPROACH

In Chapter 13, B. F. Skinner argued that people's behavior was the result of conditioning they experienced from their environment. Thus, the reinforcers or rewards in the human and physical part of our environment shape our behavior. As you will see, the behavior-modification approach to dealing with this type of person is very similar to the Adlerian approach but with a few additions.

First, keep in mind the two-step process of behavior modification. Step 1: Identify the behavior that is desired. Step 2: Apply an appropriate reinforcer at the exact moment when the desirable behavior occurs or at the moment a behavior moves in the right direction. Also, recall that positive reinforcers may be social, physical or physiological, and financial. The negative reinforcer is fear reduction. This is how behavior modification differs from Adler's approach, where the emphasis is placed on social reinforcers.

In the case of the complaining retiree, what would the desired behavior be? Perhaps it would simply be non-complaining. When does the stylist apply one of the reinforcers? When Helen isn't complaining, of course! At that time her behavior is being modified. She learns that non-complaining behavior gets her a bigger reward than complaining does. Using the two-step behavior-modification program, consider each of the five clients, find a reinforcer, and illustrate how you would use it. In a short period of time, you will help attention-seeking clients to develop more appropriate behavior in the salon.

Jean: _____

_____

_____

_____

_____

Sarah: _____

_____

_____

_____

_____

Cheryl: _____

_____

_____

_____

_____

Jim: _____

_____

_____

_____

Helen: _____

_____

_____

_____

_____

SUMMARY OF THE ATTENTION-SEEKING CLIENT

The attention-seeking client may present problems and create annoyance or even stress in a salon. This person is essentially communicating, "Unless I'm being noticed or getting attention from someone, I'm unimportant. I'll find something that will work to bring me attention." It might be a loud, boisterous attention-getting approach, or it might be a subtle, quiet one, such as sympathy seeking.

Both Adler and Skinner see the attention getter as someone who believes that acting in a certain way will get attention. Both Adler and Skinner would say that it is important to ignore the negatives. Do not reward! Instead, wait until the person shows the desired behavior or one which is in that direction; then, at that moment, reinforce. Adler reinforces with a social reward: attention, recognition, or encouragement. Skinner uses positive reinforcers that may be social, physical or physiological, financial, or the negative reinforcer of fear reduction.

Neither would use punishment. But both would agree that a matter-of-fact statement that the client is disrupting salon business and must leave can be used in those extreme cases where action becomes necessary.

You will find attention-seeking clients are the easiest to understand because you have exactly what they need — your time and your notice. Use them wisely and appropriately.

CHAPTER 18

DEFUSING THE INTIMIDATOR

The intimidator tries to show the stylist, "I know more than you do about your work, so watch out!" How can you deal with intimidators and help yourself overcome the stress they try to put on you?

Soon You Will Be Able To:

- Pinpoint the tactics of a salon intimidator!

- Constructively confront the intimidating client without destroying pride.

- Get your head together when your client tries to intimidate you.

TOUGH CLIENTS

Mary was a hairdresser who was having difficulty building clientele, and the man she married encouraged her to quit her job. Mary, now a client, was the number-one salon critic in town. As soon as she entered a new salon and a stylist started to introduce herself, Mary would point her finger at the stylist and say, "Before you pick up those shears, I want to warn you — I used to be a stylist!"

Jessica spent a month with her new in-laws in Manhattan and was treated to a coloring by one of the city's top stylists, also internationally known as a colorist. When she returned to her "old salon," she told Gina, her regular stylist, "When your hair has been colored by the best in New York City, anything after that has got to be a letdown."

Mrs. Alexander looks at and touches her stylist Gina's hair and comments, "Who does your hair? Can I get an appointment with her?"

Melinda brings a ruler into the salon and hands it to her stylist, pointing out exactly how much she wants cut off. After the cut, Melinda picks up the hair off the floor and measures a few of the trimmings. Finding a few strands a little longer than she requested, Melinda starts screaming at her stylist in the crowded salon.

Mary, Jessica, Mrs. Alexander, and Melinda are intimidators. Whether using a bulldozing style or a more subtle passive-aggressive one, all four clients present a challenge to their stylists, the kind that could result in stress. Their need to "put down" their stylist results in creating tension in the salon among staff and other clients alike. Why do people intimidate, and how can a professional cosmetologist cope with these difficult clients?

CHARACTERISTICS OF THE
INTIMIDATING CLIENT

Intimidators come in many forms. Freud would say that Mary, the former stylist turned intimidator, is using the defense mechanism called projection or trying to "project" the feelings of her own inadequacies onto others. Because she herself failed as a stylist, she now tries to find failings in all the others. You may remember that defense mechanisms operate at an unconscious level, so Mary is unaware of the motivation for her extremely critical attitude.

Jessica intimidates by being "one-up." Like the boy or girl who, on a first date, starts to brag about some of the "important" people he or she went out with before, Jessica wants to elevate herself by bragging about who did her hair. Some stylists might react by feeling inferior and then apologizing or defending themselves.

Mrs. Alexander may be intimidating but may not even be aware that she is. She is just being honest in an insensitive way when she asks her stylist, Gina, who does her hair. Many times stylists get "up tight" about this sort of insensitivity to their feelings. But keeping in mind that the world is composed of all kinds of people, and your 9:00 is one of them, will help you make it through until 10:00.

Melinda's style of intimidation is more direct — very direct as she brings her ruler into the salon. Perhaps angry from a past negative salon experience or perhaps having a need to put people down to raise her own self-esteem, Melinda, with her tough style, can very easily invite a stylist to feel intimidated. I use the word "invite" rather than cause because no client can cause a stylist to feel intimidated. To be intimidated is only one of many choices a stylist can make when confronted by a tough client. Nevertheless, some "invitations" are very strong.

Add some ways clients might try to intimidate their stylists:

_____

_____

Let's discuss some ways a stylist can respond to a disagreeable person through assertiveness and classy responding.

STYLIST ASSERTIVENESS VS. TIMIDITY AND AGGRESSIVENESS

A licensed cosmetologist or barber-stylist has every right to maintain dignity. So does everyone. When tough people, bullies, or passive-aggressives try to whittle away your rightful dignity, you, the "victim," have a right to stand up for yourself. Assertiveness is just that: maintaining one's own dignity without taking away someone else's.

There are three major approaches that people use when someone tries to erode their dignity: assertiveness, timidity, and aggressiveness. Observe the differences:

Timid Response	Assertive Response	Aggressive Response
"Die and let live."	"Live and let live."	"Live and let die."
A timid person loses her dignity while under attack.	An assertive person maintains dignity while allowing the other person the same right.	An aggressive person is uninterested in the other person's feelings and interested only in self.
Passive-aggressiveness, hurt, unsettled, desire to retaliate.	Issue is over, settled, rational thinking, new start.	Hostility, sarcasm, put down, lingering anger or fear or retaliation.
Lose - Win	Win - Win	Win - Lose

When tough people are continually aggressive with us, we have the right to respond assertively. Mary, our first tough client (the ex-hairstylist), might induce a timid reaction —

feeling bad, hurt, or passive-aggressive toward her. An aggressive hairstylist, on the other hand, might blow up and retaliate against Mary by saying, "If you think you're so hot, why couldn't you make it as a hairdresser. You had to marry someone in order to make it." Obviously Mary's dignity is being trampled by the aggressive stylist, and Mary will thus have a further need to retaliate. It could be a never-ending battle between stylist and client!

An assertive stylist might respond, "Mary, I respect you as a professional person who studied and earned her license. You can be proud of that. I'll respect your suggestions about how you would like to have your hair done, and I'll do my best for you. I want you to be satisfied as much as you do. In that way we both win, don't we?"

Both stylist's and client's dignity is maintained by assertiveness! That's just how an effective, well-balanced relationship develops.

BEING ASSERTIVE FOR THE "RIGHT" REASON (CLASSY CONFRONTATIONS)

Confrontation and assertiveness have often received bad press. Most people think that they are designed to hurt because many times they do hurt. They hurt when the intent was to hurt. They build when the motive was a positive one, however. Before asserting yourself, ask yourself what your motive is. If it isn't a constructive reason, a classy confrontation, it will be damaging to both. Consider some of the effective and ineffective motives behind an assertive confrontation:

Destructive Reason	**Constructive Reason**
To put the other person down.	To share your feelings and maintain your dignity.
To vent your anger.	To build a better relationship.
To gain one-upmanship.	To correct the situation.

EMPATHIC ASSERTIVENESS

Assertiveness is maintaining one's own dignity without

destroying another person's. Effective or classy confrontations occur when the assertive one acts from healthy motives. Assertiveness is even more effective when it is done with empathy. This is another way of preserving the other person's dignity.

You may remember that 5.0 High-Touch Empathy (Chapter 1) involves turning a person's words into feelings and offering them back to her. Let's consider this angry client and observe how a stylist responds empathically, then assertively explains the situation and shows the client the positive aspect of the situation. This is how Jessica, who had had a New York coloring, was handled:

> **Jessica:** I resent having to wait twenty minutes for a haircut. I could understand it if this salon were internationally known. My time is important.
>
> **Stylist:** It's annoying that you had to wait so long (5.0 High-Touch Empathy). I can certainly understand. It's just that the client before you needed some extra highlighting, and I think you know us well enough by now to realize that we don't want to see anyone leave without giving her the best service we can (assertive explanation).
>
> I apologize for your inconvenience. Let me reassure you that if in the future you would like some additional time, we will make it available to you (demonstrates the positive aspect of the situation, how it can benefit her).

Consider the example of Mrs. Alexander, the intimidator who asked the stylist who did her hair so that she could make an appointment with her.

> **Stylist:** Mrs. Alexander, you feel excited about my hair (5.0 High-Touch Empathy). That makes me feel good. Becky did my hair. It's a style she and I learned at a distributor's hair show a few weeks ago. I would love the opportunity to do this style for you, if you'd like. I think that you'd look just great! (assertive explanation demonstrates how a negative can be turned into a positive benefit for the client).

USING THE POWERS OF RATIONAL THINKING TO STAY UP DURING AN ATTEMPTED PUT-DOWN

As you may recall from Chapter 14 on soaring over salon stress through rational thinking, Albert Ellis shows the A-B-C System of dealing with stress, in this case attempts to intimidate. First of all, remember that people can't "cause" you to be intimidated — they can only "invite" it. You decide how it will affect you. And when you use rational thinking, you can constructively deal with the tough client.

> At <u>A</u> is some Activating Event.
> At <u>B</u> is some Belief about the Activating Event, and
> At <u>C</u> is your Consequent Emotion.

Let's consider Melinda, the client who brought the ruler into the salon to demand that the stylist cut so much off.

> **Melinda:** "I told you I wanted this much cut off and you took more. Look at this" (pointing to a hair strand she picked up off the floor). This is A, the Activating Event. The stylist now selects her Belief about the event.

> **B Irrational:** "I must be perfect; this is horrible, terrible; I can't stand it. I'm worthless." You can clearly see what her emotion at C will be — loss of self-respect, intimidation, loss of confidence, hurt, or even depression.

Now imagine the stylist using rational thinking to cope with the Activating Event:

> **B Rational:** "While I would like to be perfect and please every client, I don't need to in order to be OK because I am OK just the way I am. I'll do my best and try to improve. I can stand it, and there are hundreds of other clients that I do well."

Notice the powers of rational thinking in dealing successfully with intimidators and keeping yourself going. You Can Do It! You may even want to review Chapter 14.

SUMMARY

This chapter discussed ways of dealing with tough, intimidating clients in the salon. Some characteristics of intimidators are a need to project their own inadequacies onto others and the need to put others down in order to enhance themselves. You learned the difference between assertiveness, timidity, and aggressiveness.

You were encouraged to be assertive for the right reasons — to improve the relationship and keep your dignity while maintaining the client's as well. Empathic assertiveness is the process of (1) responding to an intimidator with 5.0 High-Touch Empathy, (2) assertively explaining the situation, and, if possible, (3) turning a negative into a positive to show benefit.

Finally, you were reminded of Albert Ellis' work on rational thinking and shown how it can be used to keep yourself going. All in all, you have now a whole toolbox of resources at your disposal when someone "invites" you to dispose of your good feelings and confidence. Remember: Anything that doesn't kill you only serves to make you stronger!

CHAPTER 19

OPENING UP
THE SHY
CLIENT

Shy clients are frustrating for hairstylists because they don't talk and they give you very few clues as to how they would like their hair designed. Not being a mind reader, how do you open up the shy client?

Soon You Will Be Able To:

- Understand the underlying reasons why some people are shy.

- Help a shy client feel more comfortable with you.

- Open up a shy client to better communication so that you can understand how she would like her hair cut.

George was a timid teenager who often brought his friend, Ernie, with him to the salon. When the stylist asked George how he wanted his hair cut, George looked up at Ernie, who answered for him. The real communication problem occurred when George came to the salon by himself.

Betty was a middle-aged, self-conscious woman who cringed when she came to the salon. She dreaded being "put on the spot" by having to answer questions from outgoing stylists. She searched through many salons to find a stylist who wouldn't ask personal questions, or, for that matter, any questions at all. Yet she never told her stylists that she preferred them to cut her hair without talking. She just left that salon and tried to find another one with a quiet stylist.

Jeanine's shyness was a designed shyness. She refused to take responsibility for communicating to her stylist how she wanted her hair done. She just said, "Do what you think," and then acted disappointed when her stylist finished. It was frustrating to work on her, to say the least!

George, Betty, and Jeanine all present difficult problems to well-intentioned stylists who want to satisfy their clients but can't because their clients won't communicate what they want. They are the shy clients, all for different motives.

Add some other behaviors you might see in shy people, e.g., body language, walk, etc:

_____

_____

_____

_____

CHARACTERISTICS OF SHY CLIENTS

In general, shy people are afraid of doing or saying something wrong. They are self-conscious or try to avoid responsibility by making others take it on. The shy ones tend to need other people's approval, overestimate the power of others, and underestimate their own. Shy clients, at first glance, seem to have some of the characteristics of the salon phobic; but there is a major difference. This person is shy in all areas of her life — at the dentist's office, school, church, and home. The salon phobic functions generally well, experiencing the symptoms of phobia only while in the salon.

Many shy people have grown up in homes where "Children should be seen but not heard!" Their parents tended to be overly critical and perfectionistic. Freud would say they have a severe superego, or conscience, thus making themselves their own worst enemies. Adler would say shy clients are discouraged and that the *purpose* of shyness is either to avoid making a mistake or to enlist someone else's attention and responsibility. In Skinner's view the shy person was punished when she attempted to offer her opinion. She learned that the best way to avoid getting hurt was to keep quiet. The encouragement system suggests that a shy person needs courage to express herself. It is possible for her to develop this in the stylist-client relationship.

George uses his friend Ernie to take the responsibility for communicating with his stylist. Ernie doesn't care because his attitude toward life is "You win some; you lose some." George trusts Ernie, and that same trust can be developed with a stylist. When George sees that a stylist is in tune with him and respects him, he will start to open up.

Betty doesn't want to reveal herself and her private life. She is self-conscious and doesn't want to get close to anyone. She may be saying, "If you get too close to me, you'll see what a horrible person I am." So she feels very uncomfortable with any communication at all. Betty probably has a difficult time building relationships in her personal life. Chances are she is a loner . . . and prefers to be that way. Betty has probably had some negative experiences with people in her past and has retreated into shyness.

Jeanine is the most difficult shy client to deal with. Her behavior is what psychologists refer to as "passive-aggressive." Her parents might have been domineering, and Jeanine felt very controlled by them and developed a shy, passive style. Her internal anger at them came out in "get back" ways. Because she couldn't express her honest feelings, she would smile, and then retaliate by doing the things that annoyed them most — leaving her clothes on the floor or getting sick at times when they were all ready to go out to a big event. The passive-aggressive client leaves a stylist feeling confused: On the one hand the stylist has a gut feeling of anger toward this client, but, on the other hand, she can't figure out why. Anger and guilt are two fluctuating emotions that a stylist has toward clients who use passive-aggressiveness.

Incidentally, people in general tend to develop passive-aggressive ways of getting back at those who try to dominate them, won't listen to their honest feelings, or have power over them. Their way of retaliating is to make them feel guilty and assume responsibility, then subtly point out their mistakes.

OPENING UP THE SHY CLIENT THROUGH BEHAVIOR MODIFICATION

You may recall B.F. Skinner's ideas on behavior modification. Skinner argued that environment shapes behavior. A stylist, as part of a client's environment, can shape more appropriate behavior by using behavior-modification techniques. The rewards (positive reinforcers) used to shape behavior are social, physical or physiological, and financial. A negative reinforcer is fear reduction. These are the appropriate reinforcers to use to reach a shy client.

The two-step process of behavior modification involves first identifying the desired behavior and then applying the appropriate reinforcer at the exact moment when that desired behavior occurs. What a stylist might like to see a shy client do may be either to speak up or to take responsibility for how she wants her hair done.

A person who usually says only "Yes" or "No" will one day say a sentence. This is desired behavior and, with reinforcement at that moment, will occur again. So the stylist reinforces with a smile, a touch, a warm glance, an "Ah-ha" with a nodding head. If a client takes a risk and hints a little at how she would like her hair cut, the stylist uses the negative reinforcer of fear reduction. She smiles and reassures with a "Nice to meet someone who knows what she wants. I think you'd look great with a new cut, too!"

In George's case, nodding his head is a form of communication and responsibility taking. That is the moment to apply the reinforcer. For Betty, reinforcement involves not putting her on the spot but allowing her to blossom at her own pace. When she does, reinforce her behavior. Jeanine needs to be reinforced by showing her pictures of a lot of different hairstyles and responding to the ones *she* likes best or the ones she doesn't like. Reinforce even the smallest indication of her decision-making attempt.

By using behavior modification, you will find in a short period of time that clients are growing and taking on more responsibility. You will have richer communication with them, especially when you add High-Touch Empathy!

SUMMARY OF OPENING UP THE SHY CLIENT

Shy people present problems to caring stylists who want to satisfy their clients. Because communication is lacking, stylists are left up in the air about how to proceed with the reticent client in the chair.

Shyness usually results from fear of saying or doing something wrong, fear of taking responsibility, or fear of retaliation. Shyness may be seen in quietness or passive-aggressiveness, in which the client refuses to say how she wants her hair done and then disapproves of what the stylist has chosen.

Behavior modification is the suggested approach to open up the shy client by first identifying the desired behavior and then applying the reinforcer at the moment it occurs. High-Touch Empathy is an excellent quality to have for creating a good, healthy, safe relationship that helps your client feel comfortable. Encouragement by communicating respect for her and noticing her good points is also of great help in loosening up the shy client.

CHAPTER 20

COPING WITH COMPULSIVE AND PERFECTIONISTIC CLIENTS

Compulsive and perfectionistic clients are rigid people, often nit-pickers, who have standards that are very difficult to meet. What are some ways of satisfying this hard-to-satisfy client?

Soon You Will Be Able To:

- Understand why some people panic at the thought of any change.

- Encourage a compulsive or perfectionistic client to relax and feel comfortable with a new look.

- Use ten different approaches to cope with the rigid personality.

Mrs. Crankshaft panics at the slightest change. She has a standing appointment every Thursday at ten o'clock. She wears only black dresses and gets upset whenever there is a change in any salon routine. When the chair she usually sat in broke down, she had to sit at another styling station. She mumbled throughout the shampoo and set about how much better she liked "her old chair." The week her regular stylist was on vacation, Mrs. Crankshaft seemed to take it personally, almost as if it were a rejection. She wants everything to be totally predictable. Rumor had it that the new salon owner had been asked by the staff please not to change the name of the salon because Mrs. Crankshaft couldn't handle it!

It is 1988, but Helen won't even consider having her stylist do anything but a beehive hairdo, which she has worn since the good old high school days when the boys chased her. Her stylist is frustrated but complies, asking Helen only one favor — not to tell anyone who does her hair!

Carmella is never satisfied. Every hair has to be perfectly in place or she explodes at her stylist. Even though she continually complains, she keeps returning every six weeks for her haircut. She always demands the same stylist, whom she sometimes keeps an extra hour until every hair is perfect.

Mrs. Crankshaft, Helen, and Carmella are either perfectionistic or compulsive clients and, as you can imagine, are a real challenge to anyone.

COMPULSIVE AND PERFECTIONISTIC CHARACTERISTICS

Compulsive and perfectionistic people have many similarities, so both types will be addressed here. The basic difference between the two is that compulsive people need exact routines and total predictability while perfectionistic people feel that unless they are perfect, they are worthless.

Freud talked about the unconscious mind being comprised of the id (I want now), the ego (the decision maker), and the superego (the conscience). Both compulsive and perfectionistic people have harsh, demanding superegos which make great demands on their egos. These demands frequently result in psychosomatic symptoms, such as migraines, ulcers, hypertension, and some forms of eczema. The harsh superego makes unrealistic demands on the person herself and on others around her. No matter how well things go for a compulsive or perfectionistic person, she is still unsettled, wondering, and worrying about some unpredictable or imperfect happening in the future.

Mrs. Crankshaft is a compulsive who needs total certainty. She must wear the same clothing, have an appointment at the same time each week, see "her" stylist, and always wear her hair exactly the same way. If there is any hint of change, her superego panics and she experiences much anxiety — which translates to her stylist as annoying behavior. Uncertainty from Mrs. Crankshaft's perspective, however, is painful.

Helen-with-the-beehive experiences the same rigid tendencies by living in the "safe," predictable past. Rollo May, as you may recall from Chapter 11 on client anxiety and resistance to change, would probably suggest stressing the *excitement* of new possibilities. Yes, anxiety is always present in change, but anxiety has positive as well as negative components. Helen, like Mrs. Crankshaft, is afraid of the uncertainties of change and panics at the thought of it.

Carmella is never satisfied with herself and her appearance. No matter how hard a stylist works on her, she just can't be satisfied. Dr. Maxwell Maltz, founder of the self-image system, would probably feel that Carmella's self-image is low and magnifies over and over again every flaw she has. She is plagued by a harsh superego. Adler would believe that she is perfectionistic to cover up for feelings of inferiority.

Add some other behaviors which give you a clue that a person may be compulsive or perfectionistic:

_____

_____

_____

_____

_____

COPING WITH COMPULSIVE AND PERFECTIONISTIC PEOPLE

Many stylists get themselves extremely up tight — that's understandable — over these types of people. The demanding client may be pushy, sometimes even aggressive, and can be quite frustrating. But it is helpful for the stylist to remember her learnings from Salon Psychology: The client's compulsive or perfectionistic demands spring from her own internal stress. In most cases they are not due to the stylist's inadequacies or inabilities.

It is also helpful to understand the underlying dynamics of the client's personality and respond appropriately. The more rigid the person, the more she suffers from the anxiety of uncertainty; the more she can't let go, the more she pushes herself. This serves, as well, to increase her pain and tensions. Someone who needs a guarantee of total predictability is essentially feeling, "Unless everything is working out as planned (same seat, same time, same stylist), it means my whole world is falling apart." To understand that emotion, imagine a time when you found yourself in a freaky, chaotic, unpredictable, twilight-zonish situation. Now magnify what you felt a few hundred times, and you will see how the compulsive person feels.

Here are ten ways in which you, the stylist, may help the compulsive or perfectionistic client:

1. **Give generous reassurance to the compulsive person.** "Mrs. Crankshaft, our chair is broken today, but we will have it fixed by next week. This other chair is just like your old one."

2. **Show the client you understand her concerns and anxieties through 5.0 High-Touch Empathy.** Reflect her feelings. "Carmella, it's probably frustrating for you when your hair doesn't turn out perfectly."

3. **Show that you will do everything possible for her.** "And so, Carmella, we are going to make this the best we can." Have you ever noticed that you rarely lose perfectionistic or compulsive clients? Why? Remember they fear change and need predictability. It will take a lot for them to risk going to another salon.

4. **Show the positive aspects of the anxiety of change.** "Sure, Helen, a new look might be different, but different is good more often than not, especially in the changing world of fashion. Let's just experiment a little and see what you think if I try just a small change here. I'll keep _____ and _____ exactly the same."

5. **Whenever possible, prepare the compulsive or perfectionistic person for any changes in the salon.** "Carmella, we are going to be using a different color system that we have found to be even better."

6. **Relax the rigid person.** Remembering the harsh, unrealistic superego this person lives with, it won't hurt to massage her shoulders prior to the shampoo or cut.

7. **Have soothing music playing in the salon.** Music does soothe the savage breast!

8. **Reinforce those moments when the rigid client loosens up.** "You look great when you hang loose. You look as if you feel good, too. Go for it!"

9. **Build trust by being as predictable as possible.** It will score many points to call this client if you are running late.

10. **Don't take her perfectionistic or compulsive behaviors personally.** Remember all the inner workings of this person. You can live with them — maybe not perfectly, but tolerably. Loosen up!

SUMMARY

Two of the most difficult clients to deal with are the rigid person who may be compulsively in need of sameness and certainty and the perfectionist who needs everything to be exactly right. Behind them lies the "anxiety of not knowing" or the "anxiety of imperfection." You were reminded why these rigid personalities develop. A harsh superego makes excessive demands on the person herself, and on others. Only when things work out predictably and perfectly is she temporarily relieved from anxiety.

Through your understanding of how the mind works and through your reassurance, empathy, and encouragement, you can cope with the rigid person. Sometimes you are able to hold her hand as she dares to take a few small steps toward change and loosening up.

PART IV

MOTIVATING YOURSELF THROUGH THE POWER OF SALON PSYCHOLOGY

CHAPTER 21

100 WAYS TO KEEP YOURSELF "TURNED ON"

Remember the day you heard that you passed the licensing exam and earned the right to be called a professional cosmetologist or barber-stylist? You turned on to your future! Remember when you were hired for your first position? Remember the first client who specifically asked for you? All these were "turn on" times in the evolution of the professional that you are today. Often a stylist forgets all that she experienced along the way to earning the right to hold the shears, apply the color, and paint new dreams of beauty for someone in her chair. If you are a student, you will soon be passing through each of these proud passages.

Soon You Will Be Able To:

- Understand many reasons why you can be constantly proud of your profession.

- Turn "down days" around.

- Have the best of both worlds — good home life, good professional life.

STAYING TURNED ON TO MY PROFESSIONAL CONTRIBUTION: FIRST-OF-THE-WEEK REMINDER TO MYSELF

1. Ultimately what I do for a living is to help people feel good. I do that through my skills, my tools, and my products . . . and through my attitude. When they look good, they feel good. And I can help by using my High-Tech/High-Touch approach.

2. I realize that I don't "just cut hair," but I also give people courage, confidence, and hope. Maybe the teenager in my chair today is thinking about asking someone out for a first date. If I help him feel confident, perhaps I will have played a role in the beginning of a new and interesting relationship.

3. Can any other profession claim that it gives gifts greater than beauty, courage, confidence, and hope?

4. I touch people. Some of my clients may not be touched by anyone else in their lives. I am the only human contact, the only human warmth for them. I can't afford to be cold.

5. I can make a little child's day by telling her how pretty she is.

6. Today I can bring a smile to an elderly lady's face by listening to the same old story she tells me every week — but I'll hear it in a different way this time.

7. I can slow down that bulldozing client who comes in hostile at the world and tell her how nice she looks when she smiles.

8. I can design that young girl's hair today with the awareness that someday she will be asking me to do her hair for her wedding.

9. Hair that was genetically and environmentally determined by the history of this particular client, I can improve in an hour!

10. I can do a before-and-after of everyone I see today by observing how he or she looked when coming in and how he or she looked upon leaving. I was the difference!

11. I can suggest additional benefits to each of my clients.

12. If I have free time, I can send out thank-you cards to my clients. Imagine how they will feel!

13. Only I can choose the attitude I take toward my clients.

14. I can look forward to an educational class coming up in the future and share it with my clients. That will make them feel confident that they have a growing, turned-on stylist who will have additional skills to benefit them.

15. I am part of a network of professionals who make the world beautiful. There are more than a million of us, and every time I do something High Tech or High Touch for someone, I add to our professional image in the collective unconscious of the world.

16. I can feel proud.

17. This day I can learn to be a more effective cosmetologist for the rest of my professional career.

18. I am creative.

19. I am able to see the results of my work as soon as it's done, unlike most other professions.

20. I can change the world, client by client!

HOW TO TURN OTHER PEOPLE ON

21. I will start every conversation with my clients by saying something positive about them. I'll be the salon stimulant!

22. I can forgive someone today and start over with that person.

23. I can turn people's negative qualities into positive qualities. I can color drab hair or give bounce to dull hair.

24. With a client or another staff member, I can dream of even better ways of creating beautiful hairstyles.

25. I can say a long-deserved "Thank you" to someone who has taught me something or given me something, especially if I have taken him or her for granted.

26. I can share my caring with someone in need.

27. Instead of talking, I'll listen.

28. I can trust again.

29. Today I will give credit to others rather than take it.

30. I can help someone feel important.

31. I am determined to look beneath that tough person's hard surface and see a soft heart.

32. I can show another stylist that I feel she is really talented.

33. Rather than compete, I choose to cooperate.

34. I can turn a backbiting conversation into a positive one, thus gaining everyone's trust and respect.

35. I will sing.

36. I can write a poem to a coworker.

37. I can understand "the other side."

38. I can give the stylist next to me a big hug — for no reason.

39. I can smile enthusiastically and be the sunshine.

40. Today I will say "I love you" to someone.

HOW TO STAY TURNED ON EVEN WHEN SOMEONE TRIES TO TURN ME OFF

41. No one chooses my attitude. I don't control what people say, but I do control my reaction to it. I choose my attitude.

42. I can understand that people who say hurtful things are hurting. I don't have to hurt myself by getting bogged down in the very game I find distasteful.

43. Instead of trying to convince someone else to be happy and thereby engaging in an emotional tug of war, I will go about my own positive way and be an example.

44. Even if I don't like her mood, I can still enjoy the individual client in the chair.

45. I'll look at all of the positive aspects about myself.

46. Today I will reflect on some of the proudest achievements of my life.

47. I'll think about the three nicest things about myself.

48. I see why rejections are tough if I choose to believe that my value as a person is based upon the approval of others. However, I choose to believe rejections are helpful because they provide opportunities for sharpening my skills with people.

49. I can absolutely, totally, completely, refuse to get down — no matter what happens.

50. When I get a break, I can retreat and listen to some soft, relaxing, or uplifting music.

51. I can take a walk.

52. I can imagine where I will be in a few hours, not where I am now.

53. If the moment seems difficult, I will think of it as low clouds on the horizon, beyond which lies the sunshine. I just have to look a little higher.

54. I could compliment the person who just criticized me.

55. I can open up honest communication with other people and let them know when they are dragging me down.

56. I can ask another stylist for help with a haircut and make her feel important.

57. I'll tell people what I like about them.

58. I could buy someone a card at lunchtime.

59. I could offer my help.

60. I could let people know that when I have a positive attitude, I feel better about my life and work.

HOW TO TURN AROUND A TURN-DOWN DAY

61. This is going to be my day, no matter what!

62. I realize that *I AM ALIVE*. This is my moment in the history of the universe. Let history record how I turned this day around! I shall never, never, never give up.

63. Life will never give me more than I can handle. Apparently life really respects me today.

64. The worst anything in life can be is . . . a simple inconvenience.

65. I'm going to second-gear myself out of this rut.

66. If we can put a man on the moon, I can overcome this setback.

67. I can actually laugh at this mess. I mean a real belly roll-around-on-the-ground laugh.

68. Things could be worse. I could be going through this experience and be thirty years older!

69. I have at least as much courage now as in the most courageous moments of my life. Let me draw on it.

70. What is, is.

71. In this situation, I'll accept the things I can't change and change the things I can. I must decide what is possible and choose whether I want to do it.

72. I can take responsibility.

73. I'm making a plan to go out on the other side of this negative geography.

74. What about a nice warm bath?

75. How many free vacations could I take right here in my own town? The park, the tennis court, the movie, a walk through some rustling leaves, a new view of the sunset, a climb up to the roof, a hot-air-balloon ride in my mind. I could even select some new bedsheets or buy a wok.

76. I could write my own horoscope for today, describing my situation and what I'll learn from it.

77. I might imagine that I am the star — pick my favorite — in a movie about a particular situation. What would she do or say? What kind of movie is it? Comedy? Drama?

78. With a lift of my chin, I will fire up my determination, feel a surge in my heart, and take charge.

79. I'll grin and bear it.

80. You know, there is almost nothing that I can't do. I can choose, decide, create, invent. Because I am alive, I can make it!

HOW TO STAY TURNED ON AT HOME AND IN MY PERSONAL LIFE

81. Each day I can look at the people around me in new exciting ways.

82. I could thank people for the ordinary, everyday things they do for me.

83. Perhaps I could remember what attracted me to my friends in the first place and refresh my attitude toward them.

84. I can include others in my work.

85. I could leave notes at home so when I'm away my family will know I am still thinking of them.

86. Because our environment plays an important role in our lives, I could make some changes in my home to make it more uplifting.

87. I could read positive books. I could reaffirm my faith, either through religion or through positive thoughts.

88. I might jot down every positive quote I hear and put them up somewhere in my home.

89. I could get some positive cassettes to listen to at night.

90. I could select more carefully the TV programs I watch by imagining how they might make me feel.

91. I'll stop reading the newspaper every day if it drags me down.

92. I am going to begin setting new goals and dreams for myself, my friends, family, or home.

93. Suppose I start an advertising campaign in my house to keep reminding me of my goals? For example, if I want to lose weight I could put a sign on the refrigerator: If you don't open this door today, tomorrow, in a *small* way, you'll be better.

94. I can look at all of the things that I do have.

95. I could get enthusiastic about others around me and their lives.

96. What if I buy some roses, cook a special meal, and pretend I still have to work to win someone over?

97. I could do something foolish to make another person laugh.

98. I could give new life to a down-and-out person.

99. I will clear my head and my problems in the salon, and I won't use my family as a scapegoat.

100. I will live today as if it were my . . . very first.

SUMMARY

TURN ON to all the ways there are to meet life today. In this chapter one hundred ways were suggested; that's just to get you thinking. There are many, many more. As philosopher Bertrand Russell observed, "In the vast realm of the alive, human mind, there are no limitations." When you are turned off, or stuck, or see a limit, reopen your eyes, ears, nose, fingers, mouth, mind, and heart. Feelings and answers will surface through your senses. Everything you need to turn on is already there.

TURN ON to your possibilities and your dreams. In the next chapter you will become a *FIND-A-WAY* person, the most valuable person in the universe.

CHAPTER 22

FIND A WAY TO YOUR DREAMS

In my practice as a psychologist, I constantly wondered why
some people suddenly, at some moment of insight, really
begin to understand life. Others never experience that
illuminating moment that shapes their new future. Interested
in the biographies of successful people, I tried to study why
some made it against all odds while others let the smallest
matter send them to Cynic City for life. I thought that if I
could find the difference, maybe others who were open-
minded could be helped. I think I found it.

Soon You Will Be Able To:

- Understand what successful people know that unsuccessful people don't.

- Identify the ten rationalizations that hold people back from actualizing their potential.

- "Find a way" to your dreams.

THE SUCCESS ATTITUDE

In working with patients and studying successful people, I found three similarities between successful, happy people and unsuccessful, unfulfilled people.

1. *Successful people do not look different from unsuccessful people.* Even *after they find that moment of insight,* you can't always distinguish them by their physical appearance. I should note that many times successful people do develop a glow about them and begin looking different; but until that insight happens, they have started from the same place as everyone else.

2. *Successful people do not start off with more money than unsuccessful people.* Frequently, this is not how they end up, however.

3. *Successful people don't run into less hardship than unsuccessful ones, but they actually gain a different view of obstacles when insight hits them.*

Realizing that, in general, successful as well as unsuccessful humans have about the same amount of time on earth to make a niche, I wanted to dissect the difference between those who make the most of it and those who do not. What did I find? The difference lies in that moment when everything becomes clear about one's relationship with life and the world.

What separated successful patients from unsuccessful ones, the moment that created a new future for them, occurred at the instant they realized that *I AM NOT AN EFFECT OF LIFE; I AM A CAUSE OF LIFE.* Unsuccessful people inevitably believe they are an effect, caused by something outside of themselves, while successful people have realized that *I CAUSE. I CAUSE HOW PEOPLE SEE ME, I CAUSE MY CHOICES TO RESPOND TO LIFE, I CAUSE MY GOAL SETTING, AND I CAUSE MY DESTINY!* This is a *FIND-A-WAY* person!

BECOMING A FIND-A-WAYER

The world is divided into two kinds of people. Some give up when faced with a barrier — like rebuilding a salon's failing business or expanding their clientele. They make excuses or find fault, and they use the same amount of time as those who find a way. Find-a-wayers are worth their weight in gold: world changers, mountain climbers, and business successes. They operate from the constant conviction that all problems have solutions, and in the spirit of Winston Churchill proclaim, "If my best isn't good enough, I'll do better." They draw from their unlimited creative determination while mediocres are looking for rationalizations to explain why they can't.

In a book on Salon Psychology, it is appropriate to talk about the limiting rationalizations that people use. What is a rationalization? Psychologists define it as giving oneself and others a "good" reason instead of a "true" reason to justify behavior that isn't up to potential. Explaining that the sun was in his eyes appears reason enough to a mediocre for dropping the ball, but a find-a-wayer would probably have prepared by wearing sunglasses. The difference is winning or losing. Excusing failure to get a promotion because the boss liked someone else better at first glance appears to be a valid, even moral reason. But the find-a-wayer avoids that rationalization by recognizing that it is important to be liked by his boss if he wants to gain his trust.

TEN RATIONALIZATIONS OR EXCUSES THAT BLOCK POTENTIAL

1. It's never been done before, or I've never done it before.

2. If only I had this one other thing, I could do the job.

3. The economy is bad.

4. It's my age. I'm not the right age for that.

5. I don't have any luck. I can't get a break.

6. I don't have the educational background.

7. I'm not big enough yet.

8. I could fail. I tried it before and it didn't work.

9. My health is poor. I'm handicapped.

10. Other people do things like that, not me.

Let's explore each of these rationalizations and see how they are interpreted differently by find-a-wayers.

> **VIEW 1:** "I'm not going to limit the visions of my future by the narrow experiences of my past."

The rationalization "It's never been done before" or "I've never done it before" is easily seen through by the find-a-wayer. Almost everything you see in the world once wasn't here and had to be done a first time. In fact, almost everything that you as a human being can do today, you couldn't do when you were born. There had to be a first time. The moment you realize you are a cause, not an effect, a mental barrier opens up and gives way to a ceilingless sky of potential.

In the popular book *Mind Power,* authors Bernie Zilbergeld and Arnold Lazarus wrote:

> Before May 6, 1954, no one had ever run a mile in under four minutes; lots of runners had tried and many had come close, but there was a barrier. Many runners and scholars argued that the barrier was physiological, that human bodies simply couldn't run that fast. As Roger Bannister, the first human to break the barrier, said, "Everyone used to think it was quite impossible, and beyond the reach of any runner." But Bannister never thought this himself and prepared himself accordingly. What is perhaps even more astonishing than Bannister's own achievement is that once he proved that it could be done, others were also able to do it. By now, hundreds of runners have run a mile in less than four minutes. It is doubtful that human physiology underwent a significant

change in that period. What is far more likely is that before Bannister's accomplishment, the self-limiting notion that the four-minute mile was impossible made it impossible. Once Bannister proved it was possible, something changed in the minds of the other runners.

A similar thing happened in weightlifting. Before Vasily Alexeev lifted 501 pounds in 1970, no one had ever lifted 500 pounds over his head, and many argued that it was a physiological impossibility. But in the month after Alexeev broke the barrier, four other weight lifters lifted more than 500 pounds. By now, scores have done it. Why? The analysis of Arnold Schwarzenegger is undoubtedly correct. "They believed it was possible. The body didn't change that month. How could the body change that much? It was the same body, but the mind was different. Mentally it's possible to break records. Once you understand that, you can do it."

My friend Leif Cook, the Scandinavian entrepreneur, talks about the impossible this way: "If something is possible, it's already done. If something is impossible, then let's begin to do it." Henry Ford contended, "Believe you can or believe you can't: Either way you'll be correct."

In speaking to a graduating class, I asked the cap-and-gowned seniors, "How many of you believe that we can cure the world's hunger problems over the next five years?" Not one of them raised a hand, and I looked at them and said, "That's why we won't, because we already have a conclusion drawn about what is and isn't possible. The world needs just one optimist to get us started. Who will it be? Why not you?"

The rationalization "It's never been done before" keeps us from reaching our dreams and blocks all of the world's progress. If you think of it, there was a time only a few decades ago when there were no washing machines, airplanes, buses, satellites, McDonald's, Wendy's, Burger Kings, open-heart surgery, TV, and almost anything else you see around you today. If the world then had been composed only of pessimists, today there would still be none of those things. Our modern-day conveniences and better ways exist only because of a few who saw beyond what was and looked for what could be. As philosopher Baruch Spinoza contended, "For as long as you believe a certain task to be impossible, for that exact period of time, it will be. But the very moment you see that just because something hasn't been done before doesn't mean it can't be done in the future, that very moment your life changes and you move closer to your dreams. Look at the world as if you see no ceilings in your future."

VIEW 2: "The only part that is missing for solving the challenge I face today is in my creative mind."

To the rationalization "If only I had this one other thing, I could succeed," the find-a-wayer looks inside his or her creative mind. A peppy young college girl named Carol Johnston set herself the goal of becoming a gymnast on a university team. She was only four feet eleven inches tall — a barrier. Apart from the obstacle of size, she had only one arm — another barrier. Yet she didn't spend her time excusing, rationalizing, or blaming. She set her will-compass on course for success and worked harder. This petite mountain of inspiration concluded that having only one arm meant she had to find a way by working harder than anyone else. Her mind made up for what was missing in her body.

Competing against hundreds of other girls with two arms, she made the U.C.L.A. gymnastic team. Her success story does not end there. Carol became one of the top gymnasts in the world! Often the only missing part for finding the way to our dreams is in our mind.

VIEW 3: "I, not the economy, decide my next move."

The rationalization "I can't succeed because of the economy" reminds me of all those salons that were still successful during the Texas oil crisis and the Midwest farm crisis.

In his important book, *The Magic of Getting What You Want,* David Schwartz wrote, "Huge, prosperous businesses such as McDonald's, Ford, Kentucky Fried Chicken, and Amway were started by people with very little capital. Furthermore, all except two of the people who led the nation in modern times — Presidents Coolidge, Hoover, Truman,

Eisenhower, Johnson, Nixon, Ford, Carter, and Reagan — were born to poor or modestly well-off parents.

Often the economy doesn't destroy a business, but the attitudes that people develop about a downhill economy lead them to act in ways that cause defeat and create a self-fulfilling prophecy of failure. In 1982, a friend of mine had a successful sandwich shop in a small Pennsylvania town. In addition to the economy's slipping, a bigger restaurant opened across the street. My friend was defeated in his mind. He told me about the customers he was losing, and as he talked, we began to realize how his defeatist attitude was causing his business failure.

"You see, Lew," he said, "I knew the economy was getting bad, and then that new restaurant opened; so I immediately started cutting back on orders to prepare for the slowdown. For the last few days, I haven't had any bread or rolls left for sandwiches at supper time. As you would expect, even my regulars started going across the street because I had to turn them away."

I asked my gloomy friend, "Wait a second; are you saying that you cut back on orders because somehow or other you knew that your competition would take away your regulars? And while they were still coming to you, you couldn't serve them so they started to go across the street?"

"Yes."

"Well, perhaps that suggests that you'd better take a clearer look at your future in a more positive way and increase your orders so a customer will never have to leave disappointed. Perhaps now, in this economy, is the time to start offering specials and taking advantage of all of the new traffic that your competition is bringing into the area. Don't defeat yourself by blaming the economy. Let the economy, whether it be negative or positive, work in your favor. Don't accept the rationalization of the economy!"

To a find-a-wayer, ideas and creativity are more important than money. The only value of money is that it enables you to find and hire find-a-wayers!

VIEW 4: "I am at just the right age today!"

Find-a-wayers don't lean on the excuse of age. Can you imagine someone discovering a cure for the common cold and having people with colds asking before they use the product, "How old was the discoverer?" Age is a rationalization that blocks the go-forward spirit. John Kennedy was only 43 when he became the president of the United States. Dwight Gooden was 20 when he was perhaps the top pitcher in baseball. Numerous businesses were started by young people with fresh, new ideas who, in most cases, were discouraged by others declaring they didn't have enough experience. And yes, while it is true that experience is important (and most stylists initially are probably not ready to open up their own business), it is also true that they can learn every day on the job, regardless of how young they are.

By the same token, "too old" has been a historic excuse for not trying. As I watched Grandma Hilda on TV, at 92, on top of Japan's biggest mountain and heard her say, "This sort of climb keeps you young," my eyes were opened to the possible-at-any-age. Colonel Sanders founded Kentucky Fried Chicken after he was retired!

David Schwartz puts the question of being too old in its real perspective in his book, *The Magic of Thinking Big*. After a training session, a man told Dr. Schwartz that he was thinking of a career change, but he would have to start from scratch. At his age, 40, it would be too difficult. Schwartz asked the man when he thought a person's productive years began, and they agreed at around age 20. They also agreed that even very conservatively speaking, one's productive years end at 70. Schwartz pointed out that there are fifty years of productivity in the average person's life. The man at 40 had used up only twenty of those fifty years. He still had thirty years, or sixty percent, of his productive years left. And he was afraid of making a change!

Psychiatrist Alfred Adler was once told by a middle-aged person, "I'm too old to go to school because if I start today, it will still be four years until I earn my degree." Adler responded, "And if you start tomorrow, it will be four years and a day!"

It is a rare person who, underneath, doesn't harbor the excuse of inappropriate age. How many people feel that they are at just the right age? What is the "right" age?

Any age is right and no age is "righter" than the one you are today!

VIEW 5: "Highly motivated, persistent people attract good luck and get the breaks."

Find-a-wayers don't wait for breaks and luck; they make things happen. While writing the book, *Think Your Way to Success,* I tried a simple experiment in order to determine if there were different ways successes and failures viewed the importance of "luck." I would like to encourage you to try the same experiment. First, identify five people you consider successful in life, and jot their names down. Next, identify five people whom you consider less than successful, unhappy, and down on life, and list their names. When you do that, conduct a simple scientific experiment. To be scientific, it is important that you ask all ten people the same question.

Ask the people in your survey this question: How much of a role do you believe that luck plays in making a person successful? Then please record all ten answers so that you can scientifically analyze patterns in their responses, if any. If you find that the five you identified as successful showed a different pattern in their response from the five you identified as unsuccessful, you will have identified an attitude of the successful person toward luck.

Until you get your results, allow me to share some of the responses I received from my own interviews. First, the unsuccessful, unhappy group:

"Luck is everything. You just have to be at the right place at the right time." (Respondent: male, age 27; unemployed for three and a half years. He has not filled out a job application in two years.)

"The cards of life are stacked against you if you don't have money." (Respondent: female, age 36; former saleswoman who recently lost her position because of poor performance and missed appointments.)

"Some people just get all the breaks in life." (Respondent: male, age 19; recent college dropout.)

As you analyze these three responses, you can see that each gives luck the key role in determining success. Next, I have recorded responses to the same question from three people whom I classified as successful:

"You make your own luck." (Respondent: female, age 32; recently received an award for being one of the top ten teachers in the state of Pennsylvania.)

"It wasn't luck that I have not missed a single sales appointment in the last two years. It wasn't luck that I made sure that every single order I received from customers was promptly filled. It wasn't luck that I made it my business to take at least four sales training or motivation courses every year. It wasn't luck that I went back to school in the evenings and in less than eight years earned a bachelor's degree in business. Come to think of it, it wasn't luck that my shoes were shined and my shirts were spotless when I made my sales calls. No, it wasn't luck that made me the top salesperson last year. And it won't be luck when I do it again this year!" (Respondent: male, age 39; top salesman.)

My favorite response came from an author of fiction. He described how early in life he was discouraged from pursuing a career in writing by failure-thinkers who told him that it was impossible to get a book published unless you had either a lot of money or an "in." His response to the question of luck in success: "I concluded that waiting for luck to come to me before I did something myself was as ineffective as looking at my reflection in the mirror and waiting for it to move first. A much more effective approach to get myself to move was to start myself moving. Something interesting happened: When I moved, my reflection in the mirror followed passively."

The attitudes of failure and success became clear to me and, I trust, will become clear to you when you analyze the results of your interviews. Failures tend to believe that people become successful because of things outside of themselves. These external factors include fate, breaks, luck, superstition, or even the stars.

Successful people, on the contrary, tend to see achievement as a product of personal effort. If there is such a thing as luck, highly motivated people are the ones who, in the long haul, tend to attract it. As one philosopher said, "The best winds seem to favor the best sailors."

VIEW 6: "Backbone is more important than background."

While rationalizers look into the past to see what is missing and give up because of it, the find-a-wayer's view of the same situation is, "I am determined to learn whatever I need to learn to reach my goal. I may have to work a little harder because I don't have the formal background, but that doesn't matter. With determination, I will compensate."

President Truman, whom some regard as one of the best U.S. presidents, might not have run for the highest office in the land because he had only a high school education. That didn't stop him, and he learned what he had to learn to get the presidency.

Albert Einstein, rather than giving up after failing physics, plowed forward to learn everything he could on his own. His insights changed the world, and it is the physics developed by him the world now studies!

Thomas Edison, perhaps the greatest inventor the world has known, quit school at age 8! He sold newspapers on a street corner, but by age 9 he had subcontracted his newsstand to a younger child so he could spend each day in the library. The light bulb, the phonograph, the curling iron, and synthetic rubber are just a few of his more than a thousand inventions.

Avoid the rationalization of not having enough educational background, and remember the examples of Truman, Einstein, and Edison. Simply become determined to learn everything you need to know to reach your dream. The library door of life is always open for the determined person!

VIEW 7: "Physical size is one thing, but visionary stature is another, related only to the depths of one's mind." Find-a-wayers don't let their current size affect who they will be in the future.

In the early 1900s the National Football League was created, and a little city called Green Bay, Wisconsin, formed a team. The city had less than 20,000 people, but its size in thinking was equal to New York's, Boston's, and Chicago's. By 1957, the team moved from playing at the high school stadium and built a stadium with 58,000 seats, for a population of only 63,000! Big thinking. Every game was sold out, and a few years later the little city of Green Bay proudly won its first Super Bowl game.

At five feet five inches, Spudd Webb is the shortest basketball player in the pro's and he can dunk a ball. Size of vision is what counts. Don't be intimidated by the "big salons." Think Big! And remember, size is related to just one thing, the depth of the vision in your mind. There will never be a better time than right now to Go For It!

> **VIEW 8:** "I could never fail because no matter what happens when I act, I get knowledge, feedback, and information that make me better equipped for the future." Rationalizers don't try because they could fail. Find-a-wayers believe one fails only by failing to act.

Here is someone's life history:

He failed at business at age 31 . . .

was defeated in a legislative race at age 32 . . .

failed again at business at age 34 . . .

overcame the death of his sweetheart at age 35 . . .

had a nervous breakdown at age 36 . . .

lost an election at age 38 . . .

lost a congressional race at age 43 . . .

lost a congressional race at age 46 . . .

lost a congressional race at age 48 . . .

lost a senatorial race at age 55 . . .

failed to become vice president at age 56 . . .

lost a senatorial race at age 58 . . .

was elected president of the United States at age 60!

This was not the story of failure, but the story of a success: Abraham Lincoln.

Dr. Robert Schuller, originator of the concept of possibility thinking, asks the question, "What would you attempt to do if you knew that you could never fail?"

You cannot fail; you only receive knowledge, feedback, and results each time you act. When you fail to act, that is when you fail to get important information for your future.

> **VIEW 9:** "My health may not allow me to do some things, but that doesn't mean I can't do anything. There are many things I can do, and I will excel at them!" Rationalizers fall back on health and handicaps. Find-a-wayers assess their assets and draw from all of the resources they *do* have, and they succeed.

I'll never forget an incident that happened a few years ago as handicapped children were getting on a school bus for the first day of school. A helpful woman tried to assist a teenager up the steps. Politely he turned to her and said, "Thanks anyway, but I can see and I can walk. I have a hearing problem, but everything else I can do!" The kind woman made the common mistake of generalizing from a single problem to a general problem.

We all make the same mistake at times, thinking that because we can't do one thing on account of our health or handicap, we can't do anything at all. Nothing could be farther from the truth.

Presidents Eisenhower and Johnson had heart attacks, yet that didn't stop them from driving forward toward their dreams.

Helen Keller said, "One can never consent to creep when one has the impulse to soar!"

Stevie Wonder and Ray Charles learned to see with their fingers, their ears, and . . . their hearts. Stevie Wonder even wrote describing the birth of his little girl whom he "saw" with his own eyes, "Isn't She Lovely?"

As I watched my friend Rosie Bailey, a cerebral-palsied girl of 33 — labeled retarded, unable to read or write a word or walk — earn her college degree, I was forevermore transformed. I hold this conviction: Don't dwell on what you don't have or can't do. See what you do have, and do with full throttle the things that you can do. Only then will you be living your life fully, and your dream doesn't have to be one bit less than everything!

> **VIEW 10:** "Great things are achieved by humans just like me, who have an extraordinary determination to surmount any obstacle and the creative determination to find a way." Rationalizers believe that others, not they, are planted with seeds of achievement.

Most people make two major mistakes: They overestimate others, and they underestimate themselves. Thus, they conclude that great breakthroughs have to be made by others.

The truth is this: When you lift up your chin, look up to new dreams, and believe that you have as much right to achieve greatness as anyone, at that moment you join the rare group of doers who go forth and change the world.

Why can't you become a great hairstylist?

Why can't you become that top platform artist?

Why can't you be the person doing famous people's hair?

Somebody has to do it. . . . Why can't it be you?

IT CAN!

FIND A WAY TO YOUR DREAMS: JUST BECAUSE SOMETHING SEEMS IMPOSSIBLE DOESN'T MEAN IT CAN'T BE DONE!

At times, the concept of "impossible" has a way of intimidating even the best of us. I guess it's because impossible sounds like an absolute, unbending and immovable. In actuality, impossible is a relative term.

The impossible is relative to time. A hundred years ago if someone had said a spacecraft would fly a quarter million miles to the moon and a man would walk out and place a flag on the moon's surface, any listener would have responded, "Impossible."

The impossible is relative to technology. In the early 1980s, it was impossible to perm bleached, fragile, and high-lift tinted hair with complete confidence. New products have been developed in the interim which change that "impossible."

Yes, the impossible is relative to time and relative to technology. But mainly the impossible is relative to the individual's creative determination and Find-a-Way Spirit! The possible is defined not by what lies outside of us but by what lies inside of us. There are just two kinds of people in the world: those who use rationalizations when they look at the impossible and those who FIND A WAY across the impossible, create new standards, and proudly achieve their dreams.

When you are finding a way to your dreams, across the impossible, and you need a little encouragement, glance up at the moon and remember the flag on its surface. And say to yourself, *I WILL FIND A WAY!*

I hope you have found a way to make Salon Psychology a part of your life. I can't wait to be with you again to share new ways of growing through all of the people resources at Matrix University.

ABOUT THE AUTHOR

Dr. Lewis E. Losoncy is a psychologist, author, creator of the Field of Salon Psychology, and Dean of Matrix University. He has written seven books, including *You Can Do It, Turning People On, The Encouragement Book,* and *The Motivating Leader,* all published by Prentice-Hall. He has been featured on many TV shows and radio programs and in the print media, including *Psychology Today, The Wall Street Journal,* and *Prevention.*

"Dr. Lew," as the hairstyling profession knows him, is a licensed psychologist who earned his doctorate from Lehigh University in Bethlehem, Pennsylvania. He was professor of behavioral science at the Reading Area Community College in Reading, Pennsylvania, and served as a consultant to many companies, such as IBM and AT&T. Since 1976 he has brought his gifts of psychology into the cosmetology profession for salon professionals to "open up" when they were ready.

Dr. Lew lives in Melbourne Beach, Florida, where he likes to grow with the promise of warm morning sunshine, feel the friendship of the waving palm trees, be inspired by the dancing sea, and learn to read the future through the songs of the gulls and sea winds. But, regardless of where he is, Dr. Lew is where he wants to be.

APPENDIX: MATRIX UNIVERSITY

Matrix University is an innovative, non-traditional educational concept geared to meet your specialized needs as a salon professional. It is the first and only source in the beauty industry to offer you a complete range of courses in business, technical, creative, communication, and psychological skills. Unlike traditional learning institutions, Matrix University is unique in that every course directly relates to your career needs. The programs are offered at convenient locations worldwide.

Matrix University gives you much more than a chance for advanced education. It provides you with a warm, comfortable atmosphere where you can interact with other salon professionals who share your needs and problems. At Matrix University people treat you with respect because they know how important you are to the lives of those you make beautiful. Best of all, Matrix University helps you discover unlimited opportunities for career advancement and personal enrichment.

DEDICATED TO ADVANCING THE SALON PROFESSIONAL

Arnold M. Miller, an experienced hairstylist and salon owner, is the founder of Matrix University. Early in his career, Mr. Miller sought salon-related information that would help him build his business and became frustrated when he found there was none. He soon discovered that the only way for salons to succeed was through trial and error.

In 1980, after nearly thirty years of successful salon experience, Arnold Miller founded Matrix Essentials, Inc., a company that manufactures exclusively professional hair-care products. By that time, he was deeply committed to building the professionalism of the industry that had given so much to him. He wanted to help other stylists develop their personal potential to the fullest. Mr. Miller envisioned a place where people could get advanced education relating specifically to the salon industry. Matrix University is the fulfillment of his dream.

ABOUT THE CURRICULUM

Currently, Matrix University offers you a complete program of courses in the field of Salon Psychology, each applying psychological principles to specific areas of the salon profession. Topics range from an overview of Salon Psychology to specifics such as building clientele, developing positive people skills, and creating a sensitive atmosphere for consultations with clients. Dr. Lewis E. Losoncy serves as Dean of Salon Psychology for Matrix University.

Matrix University will also be offering complete programs in areas such as Salon Business Management, Marketing Management, and the Science of Hair and Skin Care. All courses will be taught by instructors who are experts in their areas.

BENEFITS TO YOU, THE SALON PROFESSIONAL

At Matrix University, you have the option of enrolling for any course, or you may choose to specialize in a particular program. Upon completion of all program requirements, you will receive a diploma from Matrix University. This diploma will demonstrate that you have met the highest educational standards of the salon industry. More important, you will know how to achieve greater financial rewards, be able to reach new levels of creativity, and feel tremendous personal satisfaction in your chosen career.

In order to bring Matrix University programs to as many stylists as possible, the courses are offered throughout the year at convenient locations worldwide. They are often presented in cooperation with Matrix full-service distributors. Future plans for the University include a campus where salon professionals can complete their studies at a more intensive, accelerated pace. For further information about Matrix University write to:

Matrix University
c/o Matrix Essentials, Inc.
30601 Carter Street
Solon, Ohio 44139

BIBLIOGRAPHY

Adler, Alfred. *Social Interest.* New York: Putnam, 1939.

Adler, Alfred. *Understanding Human Nature.* New York: Greenberg, 1927.

Alberti, Robert E., and Michael Emmons. *Your Perfect Right.* San Luis Obispo: Impact, 1982.

Albrecht, Karl, and Ron Zemke, *Service America: Doing Business in the New Economy.* Homewood, Ill.: Dow-Jones Irwin, 1985.

Ansbacher, Heinz, and Rowena Ansbacher. *The Individual Psychology of Alfred Adler.* New York: Basic, 1956.

Bertrand, John. *Born To Win: A Lifelong Struggle to Capture the America's Cup.* New York: Morrow, 1985.

Carlzon, Jan. *Moments of Truth.* Cambridge, Mass.: Bellinger, 1987.

Coleman, James C., and James N. Butcher. *Abnormal Psychology and Modern Life.* Glenview, Ill.: Scott, 1984.

Cousins, Norman. *Anatomy of an Illness as Perceived by the Patient: Reflections on Healing and Regeneration.* New York: Norton, 1979.

Desatnick, Robert. *Managing to Keep the Customer.* San Francisco: Jossey, 1987.

Dinkmeyer, Don, and Lewis E. Losoncy. *The Encouragement Book: On Becoming a Positive Person.* Englewood Cliffs: Prentice, 1980.

Ellis, Albert. *Reason and Emotion in Psychotherapy.* Secaucus, N.J.: Lyle Stuart, 1962.

Ellis, Albert, and Robert Harper. *A New Guide to Rational Living.* North Hollywood: Wilshire, 1975.

Ferguson, Marilyn. *The Aquarian Conspiracy: Personal and Social Transformation in the 1980s.* Los Angeles: Tarcher, 1980.

Freud, Sigmund. *The History of the Psychoanalytic Movement.* London: Hogarth, 1956.

Hall, Calvin, and Gardner Lindzey. *Theories of Personality.* New York: Wiley, 1962.

"Impossible Doesn't Mean It Can't Be Done." *Matrix Business Builder.* Spring, 1987.

Losoncy, Lewis. *The Motivating Leader.* Englewood Cliffs: Prentice, 1985.

Losoncy, Lewis. *Think Your Way to Success.* North Hollywood: Wilshire, 1982.

Losoncy, Lewis. *Turning People On: How to Be an Encouraging Person.* Englewood Cliffs: Prentice, 1977.

Losoncy, Lewis. *You Can Do It: How to Encourage Yourself.* Englewood Cliffs: Prentice, 1980.

Maltz, Maxwell. *Psycho-Cybernetics.* North Hollywood: Wilshire, 1960.

Maslow, Abraham. *The Farther Reaches of Human Nature.* New York: Viking, 1971.

Maslow, Abraham, ed. *Motivation and Personality.* New York: Harper, 1954.

May, Rollo. *Freedom and Destiny.* New York: Norton, 1981.

Naisbitt, John. *Megatrends: Ten New Directions Transforming Our Lives.* New York: Warner, 1982.

Nightingale, Earl. *Earl Nightingale's Greatest Discovery.* New York: Mead, 1987.

Peters, Tom, and Nancy Austin. *A Passion for Excellence: Leadership Difference.* New York: Random, 1985.

Peters, Tom, and Robert Waterman. *In Search of Excellence: Lessons from America's Best-Run Companies.* New York: Warner, 1984.

Rogers, Carl R. *On Becoming a Person.* Boston: Houghton, 1961.

Salk, Jonas. *Survival of the Wisest.* New York: Harper, 1973.

Schwartz, David. *The Magic of Getting What You Want.* New York: Morrow, 1983.

Schwartz, David. *The Magic of Thinking Big.* North Hollywood: Wilshire, 1962.

Skinner, B. F. *About Behaviorism.* New York: Knopf, 1973.

Weisinger, Henfrie, and Norman M. Lobsenz. *Nobody's Perfect.* New York: Warner, 1981.

Zilbergeld, Bernie, and Arnold Lazarus. *Mind Power.* New York: Little, 1987.

INDEX